THE WISDOM
OF
INSECURITY

The Wisdom
of
Insecurity

by ALAN W. WATTS

VINTAGE BOOKS
A Division of Random House
New York

CONTENTS

Preface   9

I   The Age of Anxiety   13

II Pain and Time   29

III The Great Stream   39

IV The Wisdom of the Body   55

V   On Being Aware   75

VI The Marvelous Moment   89

VII The Transformation of Life   105

VIII Creative Morality   119

IX Religion Reviewed   135

TO DOROTHY

PREFACE

I have always been fascinated by the law of reversed effort. Sometimes I call it the "backwards law." When you try to stay on the surface of the water, you sink; but when you try to sink you float. When you hold your breath you lose it—which immediately calls to mind an ancient and much neglected saying, "Whosoever would save his soul shall lose it."

This book is an exploration of this law in relation to man's quest for psychological security, and to his efforts to find spiritual and intellectual certainty in religion and philosophy. It is written in the conviction that no theme could be more appropriate in a time when human life seems to be so peculiarly insecure and uncertain. It maintains that this insecurity is the result of trying to be secure, and that, contrariwise, salvation and sanity consist in the most radical recognition that we have no way of saving ourselves.

This begins to sound like something from Alice Through the Looking Glass, *of which this book is a sort of philosophical equivalent. For the reader will frequently find himself in a topsy-turvy world in which the normal order of things seems to be completely reversed, and common sense turned inside out and upside down. Those who have read some of my former books, such as* Behold the Spirit *and* The Supreme Identity, *will find things that seem to be total contradictions of much that I have said before. This, however, is true only in some*

9

minor respects. For I have discovered that the essence and crux of what I was trying to say in those books was seldom understood; the framework and the context of my thought often hid the meaning. My intention here is to approach the same meaning from entirely different premises, and in terms which do not confuse thought with the multitude of irrelevant associations which time and tradition have hung upon them.

In those books I was concerned to vindicate certain principles of religion, philosophy, and metaphysic by reinterpreting them. This was, I think, like putting legs on a snake—unnecessary and confusing, because only doubtful truths need defense. This book, however, is in the spirit of the Chinese sage Lao-tzu, that master of the law of reversed effort, who declared that those who justify themselves do not convince, that to know truth one must get rid of knowledge, and that nothing is more powerful and creative than emptiness—from which men shrink. Here, then, my aim is to show—backwards-fashion—that those essential realities of religion and metaphysic are vindicated in doing without them, and manifested in being destroyed.

It is my happy duty to acknowledge that the preparation of this book has been made possible by the generosity of the Foundation established by the late Franklin J. Matchette of New York, a man who devoted much of his life to the problems of science and metaphysic, being one of those somewhat rare business men who are not wholly absorbed in the vicious circle of making money to make money to make money. The Matchette Foundation is therefore dedicated to the pursuit of metaphysi-

cal studies, and, needless to say, it is to me a sign of insight and imagination on their part that they have been willing to interest themselves in so "contrary" an approach to metaphysical knowledge.

ALAN W. WATTS.

San Francisco.
May 1951.

I. THE AGE OF ANXIETY

BY ALL OUTWARD APPEARANCES OUR LIFE IS A SPARK of light between one eternal darkness and another. Nor is the interval between these two nights an unclouded day, for the more we are able to feel pleasure, the more we are vulnerable to pain—and, whether in background or foreground, the pain is always with us. We have been accustomed to make this existence worth-while by the belief that there is more than the outward appearance—that we live for a future beyond this life here. For the outward appearance does not seem to make sense. If living is to end in pain, incompleteness, and nothingness, it seems a cruel and futile experience for beings who are born to reason, hope, create, and love. Man, as a being of sense, wants his life to make sense, and he has found it hard to believe that it does so unless there is more than what he sees—unless there is an eternal order and an eternal life behind the uncertain and momentary experience of life-and-death.

I may not, perhaps, be forgiven for introducing sober matters with a frivolous notion, but the problem of making sense out of the seeming chaos of experience reminds me of my childish desire to send someone a parcel of water in the mail. The recipient unties the string, releasing the deluge in his lap. But the game would never work, since it is irritatingly impossible to wrap and tie a pound of water in a paper package. There are kinds of paper which won't distintegrate when wet, but the trouble is to get the water itself into any manageable shape, and to tie the string without bursting the bundle.

The more one studies attempted solutions to problems in politics and economics, in art, philosophy, and religion, the more one has the impression of extremely gifted people wearing out their ingenuity at the impossible and futile task of trying to get the water of life into neat and permanent packages.

There are many reasons why this should be particularly evident to a person living today. We know so much about history, about all the packages which have been tied and which have duly come apart. We know so much detail about the problems of life that they resist easy simplification, and seem more complex and shapeless than ever. Furthermore, science and industry have so increased both the tempo and the violence of living that our packages seem to come apart faster and faster every day.

There is, then, the feeling that we live in a time of unusual insecurity. In the past hundred years so many long-established traditions have broken down —traditions of family and social life, of government, of the economic order, and of religious belief. As the years go by, there seem to be fewer and fewer rocks to which we can hold, fewer things which we can regard as absolutely right and true, and fixed for all time.

To some this is a welcome release from the restraints of moral, social, and spiritual dogma. To others it is a dangerous and terrifying breach with reason and sanity, tending to plunge human life into hopeless chaos. To most, perhaps, the immediate sense of release has given a brief exhilaration, to be followed by the deepest anxiety. For if all is relative, if life is a torrent without form or goal in whose flood absolutely nothing save change itself can last, it seems to be something in which there is "no future" and thus no hope.

Human beings appear to be happy just so long as they have a future to which they can look forward—whether it be a "good time" tomorrow or an everlasting life beyond the grave. For various reasons, more and more people find it hard to believe in the latter. On the other hand, the former has the disadvantage that when this "good time" arrives, it is difficult to enjoy it to the full without some promise of more to come. If happiness always depends on something expected in the future, we are chasing a will-o'-the-wisp that ever eludes our grasp, until the future, and ourselves, vanish into the abyss of death.

As a matter of fact, our age is no more insecure than any other. Poverty, disease, war, change, and death are nothing new. In the best of times "security" has never been more than temporary and apparent.

But it has been possible to make the insecurity of human life supportable by belief in unchanging things beyond the reach of calamity—in God, in man's immortal soul, and in the government of the universe by eternal laws of right.

Today such convictions are rare, even in religious circles. There is no level of society, there must even be few individuals, touched by modern education, where there is not some trace of the leaven of doubt. It is simply self-evident that during the past century the authority of science has taken the place of the authority of religion in the popular imagination, and that scepticism, at least in spiritual things, has become more general than belief.

The decay of belief has come about through the honest doubt, the careful and fearless thinking of highly intelligent men of science and philosophy. Moved by a zeal and reverence for facts, they have tried to see, understand, and face life as it is without wishful thinking. Yet for all that they have done to improve the conditions of life, their picture of the universe seems to leave the individual without ultimate hope. The price of their miracles in this world has been the disappearance of the world-to-come, and one is inclined to ask the old question, "What shall it profit a man if he gain the whole world and lose his soul?" Logic, intelligence, and reason are satisfied, but the heart goes hungry. For the heart has learned to feel that we live for the future. Science may, slowly and uncertainly, give us a better future—for a few years. And then, for each of us, it will end. It will all end. However long postponed, everything composed must decompose.

Despite some opinions to the contrary, this is still the general view of science. In literary and religious circles it is now often supposed that the conflict between science and belief is a thing of the past. There are even some rather wishful scientists who feel that when modern physics abandoned a crude atomistic materialism, the chief reasons for this conflict were removed. But this is not at all the case. In most of our great centers of learning, those who make it their business to study the full implications of science and its methods are as far as ever from what they understand as a religious point of view.

Nuclear physics and relativity have, it is true, done away with the old materialism, but they now give us a view of the universe in which there is even less room for ideas of any absolute purpose or design. The modern scientist is not so naive as to deny God because he cannot be found with a telescope, or the soul because it is not revealed by the scalpel. He has merely noted that the idea of God is logically unnecessary. He even doubts that it has any meaning. It does not help him to explain anything which he cannot explain in some other, and simpler, way.

He argues that if everything which happens is said to be under the providence and control of God, this actually amounts to saying nothing. To say that everything is governed and created by God is like saying, "Everything is up,"—which means nothing at all. The notion does not help us to make any verifiable predictions, and so, from the scientific standpoint, is of no value whatsoever. Scientists may be right in this respect. They may be wrong. It is not our purpose here to argue this point. We need only note that such scepticism has immense influence, and sets the prevailing mood of the age.

What science has said, in sum, is this: We do not, and in all probability cannot, know whether God exists. Nothing that we do know suggests that he does, and all the arguments which claim to prove his existence are found to be without logical meaning. There is nothing, indeed, to prove that there is no God, but the burden of proof rests with those who propose the idea. If, the scientists would say, you believe in God, you must do so on purely emotional grounds, without basis in logic or fact. Practically speaking, this may amount to atheism. Theoretically, it is simple agnosticism. For it is of the essence of scientific honesty that you do not pretend to know what you do not know, and of the essence of scientific method that you do not employ hypotheses which cannot be tested.

The immediate results of this honesty have been deeply unsettling and depressing For man seems to be unable to live without myth without the belief that the routine and drudgery, the pain and fear of this life have some meaning and goal in the future. At once new myths come into being—political and economic myths with extravagant promises of the best of futures in the present world. These myths give the individual a certain sense of meaning by making him part of a vast social effort, in which he loses something of his own emptiness and loneliness. Yet the very violence of these political religions betrays the anxiety beneath them—for they are but men huddling together and shouting to give themselves courage in the dark.

Once there is the suspicion that a religion is a myth, its power has gone. It may be necessary for man to have a myth, but he cannot self-consciously prescribe one as he can mix a pill for a headache. A myth can only "work" when it is thought to be truth, and man cannot for long knowingly and intentionally "kid" himself.

Even the best modern apologists for religion seem to overlook this fact. For their most forceful arguments for some sort of return to orthodoxy are those which show the social and moral advantages of belief in God. But this does not prove that God is a reality. It proves, at most, that believing in God is useful. "If God did not exist, it would be necessary to invent him." Perhaps. But if the public has any suspicion that he does not exist, the invention is in vain.

It is for this reason that most of the current return to orthodoxy in some intellectual circles has a rather hollow ring. So much of it is more a belief in believing than a belief in God. The contrast between the insecure, neurotic, educated "modern" and the quiet dignity and inner peace of the old-fashioned believer, makes the latter a man to be envied. But it is a serious misapplication of psychology to make the presence or absence of neurosis the touchstone of truth, and to argue that if a man's philosophy makes him neurotic, it must be wrong. "Most atheists and agnostics are neurotic, whereas most simple Catholics are happy and at peace with themselves. Therefore the views of the former are false, and of the latter true."

Even if the observation is correct, the reasoning based on it is absurd. It is as if to say, "You say there is a fire in the basement. You are upset about it. Because you are upset there is obviously no fire." The agnostic, the sceptic, is neurotic, but this does not imply a false philosophy; it implies the discovery of facts to which he does not know how to adapt himself. The intellectual who tries to escape from neurosis by escaping from the facts is merely acting on the principle that "where ignorance is bliss, 'tis folly to be wise."

When belief in the eternal becomes impossible, and there is only the poor substitute of belief in believing, men seek their happiness in the joys of time

However much they may try to bury it in the depths of their minds, they are well aware that these joys are both uncertain and brief. This has two results. On the one hand, there is the anxiety that one may be missing something, so that the mind flits nervously and greedily from one pleasure to another, without finding rest and satisfaction in any. On the other, the frustration of having always to pursue a future good in a tomorrow which never comes, and in a world where everything must disintegrate, gives men an attitude of "What's the use anyhow?"

Consequently our age is one of frustration, anxiety, agitation, and addiction to "dope." Somehow we must grab what we can while we can, and drown out the realization that the whole thing is futile and meaningless. This "dope" we call our high standard of living, a violent and complex stimulation of the senses, which makes them progressively less sensitive and thus in need of yet more violent stimulation. We crave distraction—a panorama of sights, sounds, thrills, and titillations into which as much as possible must be crowded in the shortest possible time.

To keep up this "standard" most of us are willing to put up with lives that consist largely in doing jobs that are a bore, earning the means to seek relief from the tedium by intervals of hectic and expensive pleasure. These intervals are supposed to be the real *living*, the real purpose served by the necessary evil of work. Or we imagine that the justification of such work is the rearing of a family to go on doing the same kind of thing, in order to rear another family . . . and so *ad infinitum*.

This is no caricature. It is the simple reality of millions of lives, so commonplace that we need hardly dwell upon the details, save to note the anxiety and frustration of those who put up with it, not knowing what else to do.

But what *are* we to do? The alternatives seem to be two. The first is, somehow or other, to discover a new myth, or convincingly resuscitate an old one. If science cannot *prove* there is no God, we can try to live and act on the bare chance that he may exist after all. There seems to be nothing to lose in such a gamble, for if death is the end, we shall never know that we have lost. But, obviously, this will never amount to a vital faith, for it is really no more than to say, "Since the whole thing is futile anyhow, let's pretend it isn't." The second is to try grimly to face the fact that life is "a tale told by an idiot," and make of it what we can, letting science and technology serve us as well as they may in our journey from nothing to nothing.

Yet these are not the only solutions. We may begin by granting all the agnosticism of a critical science. We may admit, frankly, that we have no scientific grounds for belief in God, in personal immortality, or in any absolutes. We may refrain altogether from trying to believe, taking life just as it is, and no more.

From this *point of departure* there is yet another way of life that requires neither myth nor despair. But it requires a complete revolution in our ordinary, habitual ways of thinking and feeling.

The extraordinary thing about this revolution is that it reveals the truth behind the so-called myths of traditional religion and metaphysic. It reveals, not beliefs, but actual realities corresponding—in an unexpected way—to the ideas of God and of eternal life. There are reasons for supposing that a revolution of this kind was the original source of some of the main religious ideas, standing in relation to them as reality to symbol and cause to effect. The common error of ordinary religious practice is to mistake the symbol for the reality, to look at the finger pointing the way and then to suck it for comfort rather than follow it. Religious ideas are like words—of little use, and often misleading, unless you know the concrete realities to which they refer. The word "water" is a useful means of communication amongst those who know water. The same is true of the word and the idea called "God."

I do not, at this point, wish to seem mysterious or to be making claims to "secret knowledge." The reality which corresponds to "God" and "eternal life" is honest, above-board, plain, and open for all to see. But the seeing requires a correction of mind, just as clear vision sometimes requires a correction of the eyes.

The discovery of this reality is hindered rather than helped by belief, whether one believes in God or believes in atheism. We must here make a clear distinction between belief and faith, because, in general practice, belief has come to mean a state of mind which is almost the opposite of faith. Belief, as I use the word here, is the insistence that the truth is what one would "lief" or wish it to be. The believer will open his mind to the truth on condition that it fits in with his preconceived ideas and wishes. Faith, on the other hand, is an unreserved opening of the mind to the truth, whatever it may turn out to be. Faith has no preconceptions; it is a plunge into the unknown. Belief clings, but faith lets go. In this sense of the word, faith is the essential virtue of science, and likewise of any religion that is not self-deception.

Most of us believe in order to feel secure, in order to make our individual lives seem valuable and meaningful. Belief has thus become an attempt to hang on to life, to grasp and keep it for one's own. But you cannot understand life and its mysteries as long as you try to grasp it. Indeed, you cannot grasp it, just as you cannot walk off with a river in a bucket. If you try to capture running water in a bucket, it is clear that you do not understand it and that you will always be disappointed, for in the bucket the water does not run. To "have" running water you must let go of it and let it run. The same is true of life and of God.

The present phase of human thought and history is especially ripe for this "letting go." Our minds have been prepared for it by this very collapse of the beliefs in which we have sought security. From a point of view strictly, if strangely, in accord with certain religious traditions, this disappearance of the old rocks and absolutes is no calamity, but rather a blessing. It almost compels us to face reality with open minds, and you can only know God through an open mind just as you can only see the sky through a clear window. You will not see the sky if you have covered the glass with blue paint.

But "religious" people who resist the scraping of the paint from the glass, who regard the scientific attitude with fear and mistrust, and confuse faith with clinging to certain ideas, are curiously ignorant of laws of the spiritual life which they might find in their own traditional records. A careful study of comparative religion and spiritual philosophy reveals that abandonment of belief, of any clinging to a future life for one's own, and of any attempt to escape from finitude and mortality, is a regular and normal stage in the way of the spirit. Indeed, this is actually such a "first principle" of the spiritual life that it should have been obvious from the beginning, and it seems, after all, surprising that learned theologians should adopt anything but a cooperative attitude towards the critical philosophy of science.

Surely it is old news that salvation comes only

through the death of the human form of God. But it was not, perhaps, so easy to see that God's human form is not simply the historic Christ, but also the images, ideas, and beliefs in the Absolute to which man clings in his mind. Here is the full sense of the commandment, "Thou shalt not make to thyself any graven image, nor the likeness of anything that is in heaven above; . . . thou shalt not bow down to them, nor worship them."

To discover the ultimate Reality of life—the Absolute, the eternal, God—you must cease to try to grasp it in the forms of idols. These idols are not just crude images, such as the mental picture of God as an old gentleman on a golden throne. They are our beliefs, our cherished preconceptions of the truth, which block the unreserved opening of mind and heart to reality. The legitimate use of images is to express the truth, not to possess it.

This was always recognized in the great Oriental traditions such as Buddhism, Vedanta, and Taoism. The principle has not been unknown to Christians, for it was implicit in the whole story and teaching of Christ. His life was from the beginning a complete acceptance and embracing of insecurity. "The foxes have holes, and the birds of the air have nests, but the Son of Man hath not where to lay his head."

The principle is yet more to the point if Christ is regarded as divine in the most orthodox sense—as the unique and special incarnation of God. For the basic theme of the Christ-story is that this "express image" of God becomes the source of life in the very act of being destroyed. To the disciples who tried to cling to his divinity in the form of his human individuality he explained, "Unless a grain of corn fall into the ground and die, it remains alone. But if it dies, it brings forth much fruit." In the same vein he warned them, "It is expedient for you that I go away, for if I go not away the Paraclete (the Holy Spirit) cannot come unto you."

These words are more than ever applicable to Christians, and speak exactly to the whole condition of our times. For we have never actually understood the revolutionary sense beneath them—the incredible truth that what religion calls the vision of God is found in giving up any belief in the idea of God. By the same law of reversed effort, we discover the "infinite" and the "absolute," not by straining to escape from the finite and relative world, but by the most complete acceptance of its limitations. Paradox as it may seem, we likewise find life meaningful only when we have seen that it is without purpose, and know the "mystery of the universe" only when we are convinced that we know nothing about it at all. The ordinary agnostic, relativist, or materialist fails to reach this point because he does not follow his line of thought consistently to its end—an end which would be the surprise of his life. All too soon he abandons faith, openness to reality, and lets his mind harden into doctrine. The discovery of the mystery, the wonder beyond all wonders, needs no belief, for we can only believe in what we have already known, preconceived, and imagined. But *this* is beyond any imagination. We have but to open the eyes of the mind wide enough, and "the truth will out."

II. PAIN AND TIME

AT TIMES ALMOST ALL OF US ENVY THE ANIMALS. They suffer and die, but they do not seem to make a "problem" of it. Their lives seem to have so few complications. They eat when they are hungry and sleep when they are tired, and instinct rather than anxiety seems to govern their few preparations for the future. As far as we can judge, every animal is so busy with what he is doing at the moment that it never enters his head to ask whether life has a meaning or a future. For the animal, happiness consists in enjoying life in the immediate present—not in the assurance that there is a whole future of joys ahead of him.

This is not just because the animal is a relatively insensitive clod. Often enough his eyesight, his sense of hearing and smell, are far more acute than ours, and one can hardly doubt that he enjoys his food and sleep immensely. Despite his acute senses, he has, however, a somewhat insensitive brain. It is more specialized than ours, for which reason he is a creature of habit; he is unable to reason and make abstractions, and has extremely limited powers of memory and prediction.

Unquestionably the sensitive human brain adds immeasurably to the richness of life. Yet for this we pay dearly, because the increase in over-all sensitivity makes us peculiarly vulnerable. One can be less vulnerable by becoming less sensitive—more of a stone and less of a man—and so less capable of enjoyment. Sensitivity requires a high degree of softness and fragility—eyeballs, eardrums, taste buds, and nerve ends culminating in the highly delicate organism of the brain. These are not only soft and fragile, but also perishable. There seems to be no effective way of decreasing the delicacy and perishability of living tissue without also decreasing its vitality and sensitivity.

If we are to have intense pleasures, we must also be liable to intense pains. The pleasure we love, and the pain we hate, but it seems impossible to have the former without the latter. Indeed, it looks as if the two *must* in some way alternate, for continuous pleasure is a stimulus that must either pall or be increased. And the increase will either harden the sense buds with its friction, or turn into pain. A consistent diet of rich food either destroys the appetite or makes one sick.

To the degree, then, that life is found good, death must be proportionately evil. The more we are able to love another person and to enjoy his company, the greater must be our grief at his death, or in separation. The further the power of consciousness ventures out into experience, the more is the price it must pay for its knowledge. It is understandable that we should sometimes ask whether life has not gone too far in this direction, whether "the game is worth the candle," and whether it might not be better to turn the course of evolution in the only other possible direction—backwards, to the relative peace of the animal, the vegetable, and the mineral.

Something of this kind is often attempted. There is the woman who, having suffered some deep emotional injury in love or marriage, vows never to let another man play on her feelings, assuming the role of the hard and bitter spinster. Almost more common is the sensitive boy who learns in school to encrust himself for life in the shell of the "tough-guy" attitude. As an adult he plays, in self-defense, the role of the Philistine, to whom all intellectual and emotional culture is womanish and "sissy." Carried to its final extreme, the logical end of this type of reaction to life is suicide. The hard-bitten kind of person is always, as it were, a partial suicide; some of himself is already dead.

If, then, we are to be fully human and fully alive and aware, it seems that we must be willing to suffer for our pleasures. Without such willingness there can be no growth in the intensity of consciousness. Yet, generally speaking, we are not willing, and it may be thought strange to suppose that we can be. For "nature in us" so rebels against pain that the very notion of "willingness" to put up with it beyond a certain point may appear impossible and meaningless.

Under these circumstances, the life that we live is a contradiction and a conflict. Because consciousness *must* involve both pleasure and pain, to strive for pleasure to the exclusion of pain is, in effect, to strive for the loss of consciousness. Because such a loss is in principle the same as death, this means that the more we struggle for life (as pleasure), the more we are actually killing what we love.

Indeed, this is the common attitude of man to so much that he loves. For the greater part of human activity is designed to make permanent those experiences and joys which are only lovable because they are changing. Music is a delight because of its rhythm and flow. Yet the moment you arrest the flow and prolong a note or chord beyond its time, the rhythm is destroyed. Because life is likewise a flowing process, change and death are its necessary parts. To work for their exclusion is to work against life.

However, the simple experiencing of alternating pain and pleasure is by no means the heart of the human problem. The reason that we want life to mean something, that we seek God or eternal life, is not merely that we are trying to get away from an immediate experience of pain. Nor is it for any such reason that we assume attitudes and roles as habits of perpetual self-defense. The real problem does not come from any momentary sensitivity to pain, but from our marvelous powers of memory and foresight—in short from our consciousness of *time*.

For the animal to be happy it is enough that this moment be enjoyable. But man is hardly satisfied with this at all. He is much more concerned to have enjoyable memories and expectations — especially the latter. With these assured, he can put up with an extremely miserable present. Without this assurance, he can be extremely miserable in the midst of immediate physical pleasure.

Here is a person who knows that in two weeks' time he has to undergo a surgical operation. In the meantime he is feeling no physical pain; he has plenty to eat; he is surrounded by friends and human affection; he is doing work that is normally of great interest to him. But his power to enjoy these things is taken away by constant dread. He is insensitive to the immediate realities around him. His mind is preoccupied with something that is not yet here. It is not as if he were thinking about it in a practical way, trying to decide whether he should have the operation or not, or making plans to take care of his family and his affairs if he should die. These decisions have already been made. Rather, he is thinking about the operation in an entirely futile way, which both ruins his present enjoyment of life and contributes nothing to the solution of any problem. But he cannot help himself.

This is the typical human problem. The object of dread may not be an operation in the immediate future. It may be the problem of next month's rent, of a threatened war or social disaster, of being able to save enough for old age, or of death at the last. This "spoiler of the present" may not even be a future dread. It may be something out of the past, some memory of an injury, some crime or indiscretion, which haunts the present with a sense of resentment or guilt. The power of memories and expectations is such that for most human beings the past and the future are not *as* real, but *more* real than the present. The present cannot be lived happily unless the past has been "cleared up" and the future is bright with promise.

There can be no doubt that the power to remember and predict, to make an ordered sequence out of a helter-skelter chaos of disconnected moments, is a wonderful development of sensitivity. In a way it is *the* achievement of the human brain, giving man the most extraordinary powers of survival and adaptation to life. But the way in which we generally use this power is apt to destroy all its advantages. For it is of little use to us to be able to remember and predict if it makes us unable to live fully in the present.

What is the use of planning to be able to eat next week unless I can really enjoy the meals when they come? If I am so busy planning how to eat next week that I cannot fully enjoy what I am eating *now*, I will be in the same predicament when next week's meals become "now."

If my happiness at this moment consists largely in reviewing happy memories and expectations, I am but dimly aware of this present. I shall still be dimly aware of the present when the good things that I have been expecting come to pass. For I shall have formed a habit of looking behind and ahead, making it difficult for me to attend to the here and now. If, then, my awareness of the past and future makes me less aware of the present, I must begin to wonder whether I am actually living in the real world.

After all, the future is quite meaningless and unimportant unless, sooner or later, it is going to become the present. Thus to plan for a future which is not going to become present is hardly more absurd than to plan for a future which, when it comes to me, will find me "absent," looking fixedly over its shoulder instead of into its face.

This kind of living in the fantasy of expectation rather than the reality of the present is the special trouble of those business men who live entirely to make money. So many people of wealth understand much more about making and saving money than about using and enjoying it. They fail to live because they are always preparing to live. Instead of earning a living they are mostly earning an earning, and thus when the time comes to relax they are unable to do so. Many a "successful" man is bored and miserable when he retires, and returns to his work only to prevent a younger man from taking his place.

From still another point of view the way in which we use memory and prediction makes us less, rather than more, adaptable to life. If to enjoy even an enjoyable present we *must* have the assurance of a happy future, we are "crying for the moon." We have no such assurance. The best predictions are still matters of probability rather than certainty, and to the best of our knowledge every one of us is going to suffer and die. If, then, we cannot live happily without an assured future, we are certainly not adapted to living in a finite world where, despite the best plans, accidents will happen, and where death comes at the end.

This, then, is the human problem: there is a price to be paid for every increase in consciousness. We cannot be more sensitive to pleasure without being more sensitive to pain. By remembering the past we can plan for the future. But the ability to plan for pleasure is offset by the "ability" to dread pain and to fear the unknown. Furthermore, the growth of an acute sense of the past and the future gives us a correspondingly dim sense of the present. In other words, we seem to reach a point where the advantages of being conscious are outweighed by its disadvantages, where extreme sensitivity makes us unadaptable.

Under these circumstances we feel in conflict with our own bodies and the world around them, and it is consoling to be able to think that in this contradictory world we are but "strangers and pilgrims." For if our desires are out of accord with anything that the finite world can offer, it might seem that our nature is not of this world, that our hearts are made, not for the finite, but for infinity. The discontent of our souls would appear to be the sign and seal of their divinity.

But does the desire for something prove that the thing exists? We know that it does not necessarily do so at all. It may be consoling to think that we are citizens of another world than this, and that after our exile upon earth we may return to the true home of our heart's desire. But if we *are* citizens of this world, and if there can be no final satisfaction of the soul's discontent, has not nature, in bringing forth man, made a serious mistake?

For it would seem that, in man, life is in hopeless conflict with itself. To be happy, we must have what we cannot have. In man, nature has conceived desires which it is impossible to satisfy. To drink more fully of the fountain of pleasure, it has brought forth capacities which make man the more susceptible to pain. It has given us the power to control the future but a little—the price of which is the frustration of knowing that we must at last go down in defeat. If we find this absurd, this is only to say that nature has conceived intelligence in us to berate itself for absurdity. Consciousness seems to be nature's ingenious mode of self-torture.

Of course we do not want to think that this is true. But it would be easy to show that most reasoning to the contrary is but wishful thinking—nature's method of putting off suicide so that the idiocy can continue. Reasoning, then, is not enough. We must go deeper. We must look into this life, this nature, which has become aware within us, and find out whether it is really in conflict with itself, whether it *actually* desires the security and the painlessness which its individual forms can never enjoy.

III. THE GREAT STREAM

WE SEEM TO BE LIKE FLIES CAUGHT IN HONEY. BE-cause life is sweet we do not want to give it up, and yet the more we become involved in it, the more we are trapped, limited, and frustrated. We love it and hate it at the same time. We fall in love with people and possessions only to be tortured by anxiety for them. The conflict is not only between ourselves and the surrounding universe; it is between ourselves and ourselves. For intractable nature is both around and within us. The exasperating "life" which is at once lovable and perishable, pleasant and pain-ful, a blessing and a curse, is also the life of our own bodies.

It is as if we were divided into two parts. On the one hand there is the conscious "I," at once intrigued and baffled, the creature who is caught in the trap. On the other hand there is "me," and "me" is a part of nature—the wayward flesh with all its concur-rently beautiful and frustrating limitations. "I" fan-cies itself as a reasonable fellow, and is forever crit-icizing "me" for its perversity—for having passions which get "I" into trouble, for being so easily sub-ject to painful and irritating diseases, for having or-gans that wear out, and for having appetites which can never be satisfied—so designed that if you try to allay them finally and fully in one big "bust," you get sick.

Perhaps the most exasperating thing about "me," about nature and the universe, is that it will never "stay put." It is like a beautiful woman who will never be caught, and whose very flightiness is her charm. For the perishability and changefulness of the world is part and parcel of its liveliness and loveliness. This is why the poets are so often at their best when speaking of change, of "the transitoriness of human life." The beauty of such poetry lies in something more than a note of nostalgia which brings a catch in the throat.

> *Our revels now are ended. These our actors,*
> *As I foretold you, were all spirits, and*
> *Are melted into air, into thin air:*
> *And, like the baseless fabric of this vision,*
> *The cloud-capp'd towers, the gorgeous palaces,*
> *The solemn temples, the great globe itself,*
> *Yea, all which it inherit, shall dissolve,*
> *And, like this insubstantial pageant faded,*
> *Leave not a rack behind.*

There is more in this beauty than the succession of melodious images, and the theme of dissolution does not simply borrow its splendor from the things dissolved. The truth is rather that the images, though beautiful in themselves, come to life in the act of vanishing. The poet takes away their static solidity, and turns a beauty which would otherwise be only statuesque and architectural into music, which, no sooner than it is sounded, dies away. The towers, palaces, and temples become vibrant, and break from the excess of life within them. To be passing is to live; to remain and continue is to die. "Unless a grain of corn fall into the ground and die, it remains alone. But if it dies, it brings forth much fruit."

For the poets have seen the truth that life, change, movement, and insecurity are so many names for the same thing. Here, if anywhere, truth is beauty, for movement and rhythm are of the essence of all things lovable. In sculpture, architecture, and painting the finished form stands still, but even so the eye finds pleasure in the form only when it contains a certain lack of symmetry, when, frozen in stone as it may be, it looks as if it were in the midst of motion.

Is it not, then, a strange inconsistency and an unnatural paradox that "I" resists change in "me" and in the surrounding universe? For change is not merely a force of destruction. Every form is really a pattern of movement, and every living thing is like the river, which, if it did not flow out, would never have been able to flow in. Life and death are not two opposed forces; they are simply two ways of looking at the same force, for the movement of change is as much the builder as the destroyer. The human body lives because it is a complex of motions, of circulation, respiration, and digestion. To resist change, to try to cling to life, is therefore like holding your breath: if you persist you kill yourself.

In thinking of ourselves as divided into "I" and "me," we easily forget that consciousness also lives because it is moving. It is as much a part and product of the stream of change as the body and the whole natural world. If you look at it carefully, you will see that consciousness—the thing you call "I"—is really a stream of experiences, of sensations, thoughts, and feelings in constant motion. But because these experiences include memories, we have the impression that "I" is something solid and still, like a tablet upon which life is writing a record.

Yet the "tablet" moves with the writing finger as the river flows along with the ripples, so that memory is like a record written on water—a record, not of graven characters, but of waves stirred into motion by other waves which are called sensations and facts. The difference between "I" and "me" is largely an illusion of memory. In truth, "I" is of the same nature as "me." It is part of our whole being, just as the head is part of the body. But if this is not realized, "I" and "me," the head and the body, will feel at odds with each other. "I," not understanding that it too is part of the stream of change, will try to make sense of the world and experience by attempting to *fix* it.

We shall then have a war between consciousness and nature, between the desire for permanence and the fact of flux. This war must be utterly futile and frustrating—a vicious circle—because it is a conflict between two parts of the same thing. It must lead thought and action into circles which go nowhere faster and faster. For when we fail to see that our life *is* change, we set ourselves against ourselves and become like Ouroboros, the misguided snake, who tries to eat his own tail. Ouroboros is the perennial symbol of all vicious circles, of every attempt to split our being asunder and make one part conquer the other.

Struggle as we may, "fixing" will never make sense out of change. The only way to make sense out of change is to plunge into it, move with it, and join the dance.

Religion, as most of us have known it, has quite obviously tried to make sense out of life by fixation. It has tried to give this passing world a meaning by relating it to an unchanging God, and by seeing its goal and purpose as an immortal life in which the individual becomes one with the changeless nature of the deity. "Rest eternal grant unto them, O Lord, and let light perpetual shine upon them." Likewise, it attempts to make sense out of the swirling movements of history by relating them to the fixed laws of God, "whose Word endureth for ever."

We have thus made a problem for ourselves by confusing the intelligible with the fixed. We think that making sense out of life is impossible unless the flow of events can somehow be fitted into a framework of rigid forms. To be meaningful, life must be understandable in terms of fixed ideas and laws, and these in turn must correspond to unchanging and eternal realities behind the shifting scene.[1] But if this is what "making sense out of life" means, we have set ourselves the impossible task of making fixity out of flux.

Before we can find out whether there is some better way of understanding our universe, we must see clearly how this confusion of "sense" with "fixity" has come about.

The root of the difficulty is that we have developed the power of thinking so rapidly and one-sidedly that we have forgotten the proper relation between thoughts and events, words and things. Conscious thinking has gone ahead and created its own world, and, when this is found to conflict with the real world, we have the sense of a profound discord between "I," the conscious thinker, and nature. This one-sided development of man is not peculiar to intellectuals and "brainy" people, who are only extreme examples of a tendency which has affected our entire civilization.

What we have forgotten is that thoughts and words are *conventions,* and that it is fatal to take conven-

[1] Later on in this book we shall see that these metaphysical ideas of the unchanging and the eternal can have another sense. They do not necessarily imply a static view of reality, and while ordinarily used as attempts to "fix the flux" they have not always been so.

tions too seriously. A convention is a social convenience, as, for example, money. Money gets rid of the inconveniences of barter. But it is absurd to take money too seriously, to confuse it with real wealth, because it will do you no good to eat it or wear it for clothing. Money is more or less static, for gold, silver, strong paper, or a bank balance can "stay put" for a long time. But real wealth, such as food, is perishable. Thus a community may possess all the gold in the world, but if it does not farm its crops it will starve.

In somewhat the same way, thoughts, ideas, and words are "coins" for real things. They are *not* those things, and though they represent them, there are many ways in which they do not correspond at all. As with money and wealth, so with thoughts and things: ideas and words are more or less fixed, whereas real things change.

It is easier to say "I" than to point to your own body, and to say "want" than to try to indicate a vague feeling in the mouth and stomach. It is more convenient to say "water" than to lead your friend to a well and make suitable motions. It is also convenient to agree to use the same words for the same things, and to keep these words unchanged, even though the things we are indicating are in constant motion.

In the beginning, the power of words must have seemed magical, and, indeed, the miracles which

45

verbal thinking has wrought have justified the impression. What a marvel it must have been to get rid of the nuisances of sign-language and summon a friend simply by making a short noise—his name! It is no wonder that names have been considered uncanny manifestations of supernatural power, and that men have identified their names with their souls or used them to invoke spiritual forces. Indeed, the power of words has gone to man's head in more than one way. To define has come to mean almost the same thing as to understand. More important still, words have enabled man to define himself—to label a certain part of his experience "I."

This is, perhaps, the meaning of the ancient belief that the name is the soul. For to define is to isolate, to separate some complex of forms from the stream of life and say, "This is I." When man can name and define himself, he feels that he has an identity. Thus he begins to feel, like the word, separate and static, as over against the real, fluid world of nature.

Feeling separate, the sense of conflict between man, on the one hand, and nature, on the other, begins. Language and thought grapple with the conflict, and the magic which can summon a man by naming him is applied to the universe. Its powers are named, personalized, and invoked in mythology and religion. Natural processes are made intelligible, because all *regular* processes—such as the rotation of the stars and seasons—can be fitted to words and ascribed to the activity of the gods or God, the eternal Word. At a later time science employs the same process, studying every kind of regularity in the universe, naming, classifying, and making use of them in ways still more miraculous.

But because it is the use and nature of words and thoughts to be fixed, definite, isolated, it is extremely hard to describe the most important characteristic of life—its movement and fluidity. Just as money does not represent the perishability and edibility of food, so words and thoughts do not represent the vitality of life. The relation between thought and movement is something like the difference between a real man running and a motion-picture film which shows the running as a series of "stills."

We resort to the convention of stills whenever we want to describe or think about any moving body, such as a train, stating that at such-and-such times it is *at* such-and-such places. But this is not quite true. You can say that a train is at a particular point "now!" But it took you some time to say "now!" and during that time, however short, the train was still moving. You can only say that the moving train actually *is* (i.e., stops) at a particular point for a particular moment if both are infinitely small. But infinitely small points and fixed moments are always imaginary points, being denizens of mathematical theory rather than the real world.

It is most convenient for scientific calculation to

47

think of a movement as a series of very small jerks or stills. But confusion arises when the world described and measured by such conventions is identified with the world of experience. A series of stills does not, unless rapidly *moved* before our eyes, convey the essential vitality and beauty of movement. The definition, the description, leaves out the most important thing.

Useful as these conventions are for purposes of calculation, language, and logic, absurdities arise when we think that the kind of language we use or the kind of logic with which we reason can really define or explain the "physical" world. Part of man's frustration is that he has become accustomed to expect language and thought to offer explanations which they cannot give. To want life to be "intelligible" in this sense is to want it to be something other than life. It is to prefer a motion-picture film to a real, running man. To feel that life is meaningless unless "I" can be permanent is like having fallen desperately in love with an inch.

Words and measures do not give life; they merely symbolize it. Thus all "explanations" of the universe couched in language are circular, and leave the most essential things unexplained and undefined. The dictionary itself is circular. It defines words in terms of other words. The dictionary comes a little closer to life when, alongside some word, it gives you a picture. But it will be noted that all dictionary pictures are attached to nouns rather than verbs. An illustration of the verb *to run* would have to be a series of stills like a comic strip, for words and static pictures can neither define nor explain a motion.

Even the nouns are conventions. You do not define this real, living "something" by associating it with the noise *man*. When we say, "This (pointing with the finger) *is* a man," the thing to which we point is not *man*. To be clearer we should have said, "This is symbolized by the noise *man*." What, then, is *this*? We do not know. That is to say, we cannot define it in any fixed way, though, in another sense, we know it as our immediate experience—a flowing process without definable beginning or end. It is convention alone which persuades me that I am simply this body bounded by a skin in space, and by birth and death in time.

Where do I begin and end in space? I have relations to the sun and air which are just as vital parts of my existence as my heart. The movement in which I am a pattern or convolution began incalculable ages before the (conventionally isolated) event called birth, and will continue long after the event called death. Only words and conventions can isolate us from the entirely undefinable something which is everything.

Now these are useful words, so long as we treat them as conventions and use them like the imaginary lines of latitude and longitude which are drawn upon maps, but are not actually found upon the face of the earth. But in practice we are all bewitched by words. We confuse them with the real world, and try to live in the real world as if it were the world of words. As a consequence, we are dismayed and dumbfounded when they do not fit. The more we try to live in the world of words, the more we feel isolated and alone, the more all the joy and liveliness of things is exchanged for mere certainty and security. On the other hand, the more we are forced to admit that we actually live in the real world, the more we feel ignorant, uncertain, and insecure about everything.

But there can be no sanity unless the difference between these two worlds is recognized. The scope and purposes of science are woefully misunderstood when the universe which it describes is confused with the universe in which man lives. Science is talking about a symbol of the real universe, and this symbol has much the same use as money. It is a convenient timesaver for making practical arrangements. But when money and wealth, reality and science are confused, the symbol becomes a burden.

Similarly, the universe described in formal, dogmatic religion is nothing more than a symbol of the real world, being likewise constructed out of verbal and conventional distinctions. To separate "this person" from the rest of the universe is to make a conventional separation. To want "this person" to be eternal is to want the words to be the reality, and to insist that a convention endure for ever and ever. We hunger for the perpetuity of something which never existed. Science has "destroyed" the religious symbol of the world because, when symbols are confused with reality, different ways of symbolizing reality will seem contradictory.

The scientific way of symbolizing the world is more suited to utilitarian purposes than the religious way, but this does not mean that it has any more "truth." Is it truer to classify rabbits according to their meat or according to their fur? It depends on what you want to do with them. The clash between science and religion has not shown that religion is false and science is true. It has shown that all systems of definition are relative to various purposes, and that none of them actually "grasp" reality. And because religion was being misused as a means for actually grasping and possessing the mystery of life, a certain measure of "debunking" was highly necessary.

But in the process of symbolizing the universe in this way or that for this purpose or that we seem to have lost the actual joy and meaning of life itself. All the various definitions of the universe have had ulterior motives, being concerned with the future rather than the present. Religion wants to assure the future beyond death, and science wants to assure it until death, and to postpone death. But tomorrow and plans for tomorrow can have no significance at all unless you are in full contact with the reality of the present, since it is in the present and *only* in the present that you live. There is no other reality than present reality, so that, even if one were to live for endless ages, to live for the future would be to miss the point everlastingly.

But it is just this reality of the present, this moving, vital *now* which eludes all the definitions and descriptions. Here is the mysterious real world which words and ideas can never pin down. Living always for the future, we are out of touch with this source and center of life, and as a result all the magic of naming and thinking has come to something of a temporary breakdown.

The miracles of technology cause us to live in a hectic, clockwork world that does violence to human biology, enabling us to do nothing but pursue the future faster and faster. Deliberate thought finds itself unable to control the upsurge of the beast in man —a beast more "beastly" than any creature of the wild, maddened and exasperated by the pursuit of illusions. Specialization in verbiage, classification, and mechanized thinking has put man out of touch with many of the marvelous powers of "instinct" which govern his body. It has, furthermore, made him feel utterly separate from the universe and his own "me." And thus when all philosophy has dissolved in relativism, and can make fixed sense of the universe no longer, isolated "I" feels miserably insecure and panicky, finding the real world a flat contradiction of its whole being.

Of course there is nothing new in this predicament of discovering that ideas and words cannot plumb the ultimate mystery of life, that Reality or, if you will, God cannot be comprehended by the finite mind. The only novelty is that the predicament is now social rather than individual; it is widely felt, not confined to the few. Almost every spiritual tradition recognizes that a point comes when two things must happen: man must surrender his separate-feeling "I," and must face the fact that he cannot know, that is, define the ultimate.

These traditions also recognize that beyond this point there lies a "vision of God" which cannot be put into words, and which is certainly something utterly different from perceiving a radiant gentleman on a golden throne, or a literal flash of blinding light. They also indicate that this vision is a restoration of something which we once had, and "lost" because we did not or could not appreciate it. This vision is, then, the unclouded awareness of this undefinable "something" which we call life, present reality, the great stream, the eternal now—an awareness without the sense of separation from it.

The moment I name it, it is no longer God; it is man, tree, green, black, red, soft, hard, long, short, atom, universe. One would readily agree with any theologian who deplores pantheism that these denizens of the world of verbiage and convention, these sundry "things" conceived as fixed and distinct entities, are not God. If you ask me to show you God, I will point to the sun, or a tree, or a worm. But if you say, "You mean, then, that God is the sun, the tree, the worm, and all other things?"—I shall have to say that you have missed the point entirely.

IV. THE WISDOM OF THE BODY

WHAT IS EXPERIENCE? WHAT IS LIFE? WHAT IS MOTION?
What is reality? To all such questions we must give
St. Augustine's answer to the question, "What is
time?"—"I know, but when you ask me I don't." Experience, life, motion, and reality are so many noises
used to symbolize the sum of sensations, thoughts,
feelings, and desires. And if you ask, "What are sensations, et cetera?" I can only answer, "Don't be silly.
You know very well what they are. We can't go on
defining things indefinitely without going round in
circles. To define means to fix, and, when you get
down to it, real life isn't fixed."

It was suggested at the end of the last chapter that
this ultimate something which cannot be defined or
fixed can be represented by the word *God*. If this be
true, we know God all the time—but when we begin
to think about it we don't. For when we begin to
think about experience we try to fix it in rigid forms
and ideas. It is the old problem of trying to tie up
water in parcels, or attempting to shut the wind in a
box.

Yet it has always been taught in religion that
"God" is something from which one can expect wisdom and guidance. We have become accustomed to
the idea that wisdom—that is, knowledge, advice, and

information—can be expressed in verbal statements consisting of specific directions. If this be true, it is hard to see how any wisdom can be extracted from something impossible to define.

But in fact the kind of wisdom which can be put in the form of specific directions amounts to very little, and most of the wisdom which we employ in everyday life never came to us as verbal information. It was not through statements that we learned how to breathe, swallow, see, circulate the blood, digest food, or resist diseases. Yet these things are performed by the most complex and marvelous processes which no amount of book-learning and technical skill can reproduce. This is real wisdom—but our brains have little to do with it. This is the kind of wisdom which we need in solving the real, practical problems of human life. It has done wonders for us already, and there is no reason why it should not do much more.

Without any technical apparatus or calculations for prediction, homing-pigeons can return to their roosts from long distances away, migrant birds can revisit the same locations year after year, and plants can "devise" wonderful contraptions for distributing their seeds on the wind. They do not, of course, do these things "on purpose," which is only to say that they do not plan and think them out. If they could talk, they could no more explain how it is done than the average man can explain how his heart beats.

The "instruments" which achieve these feats are, indeed, organs and processes of the body—that is to say, of a mysterious pattern of movement which we do not really understand and cannot actually define. In general, however, human beings have ceased to develop the instruments of the body. More and more we try to effect an adaptation to life by means of external gadgets, and attempt to solve our problems by conscious thinking rather than unconscious "know-how." This is much less to our advantage than we like to suppose.

There are, for instance, "primitive" women who can deliver themselves of a child while working out in the fields, and, after doing the few things necessary to see that the baby is safe, warm, and comfortable, resume their work as before. On the other hand, the civilized woman has to be moved to a complicated hospital, and there, surrounded by doctors, nurses, and innumerable gadgets, force the poor thing into the world with prolonged contortions and excruciating pains. It is true that antiseptic conditions prevent many mothers and babies from dying, but why can't we have the antiseptic conditions *and* the natural, easy way of birth?

The answer to this, and many similar questions, is that we have been taught to neglect, despise, and violate our bodies, and to put all faith in our brains. Indeed, the special disease of civilized man might be described as a block or schism between his brain (specifically, the cortex) and the rest of his body. This corresponds to the split between "I" and "me," man and nature, and to the confusion of Ouroboros, the mixed-up snake, who does not know that his tail belongs with his head. Happily, there have, in recent years, been at least two scientists who have called attention to this schism, namely Lancelot Law Whyte and Trigant Burrow.[1] Whyte calls this disease the "European dissociation," not because it is peculiar to European-American civilization, but because it is specially characteristic of it.

Both Whyte and Burrow have given a clinical description or diagnosis of the schism, the details of which need not detain us here. It is simply saying in "medical" language that we have allowed brain thinking to develop and dominate our lives out of all proportion to "instinctual wisdom," which we are allowing to slump into atrophy. As a consequence, we are at war within ourselves—the brain desiring things which the body does not want, and the body desiring things which the brain does not allow; the brain giving directions which the body will not follow, and

[1] Of L. L. Whyte's books, *The Next Development in Man* (Henry Holt, New York, 1943) is quite readable and deeply interesting, while *The Unitary Principle in Physics and Biology* (Henry Holt, New York, 1949) is strictly for the scientific reader. Burrow's *Social Basis of Consciousness* (London, 1927) and *The Structure of Insanity* (London, 1932) are unhappily out of print, but most of the material is contained in his *Neurosis of Man* (Routledge, London, 1948). There are probably other scientists working on the same lines, but I am not aware of them.

the body giving impulses which the brain cannot understand.

In one way or another civilized man agrees with St. Francis in thinking of the body as Brother Ass. But even theologians have recognized that the source of evil and stupidity lies not in the physical organism as a whole, but in the cut-off, dissociated brain which they term the "will."

When we compare human with animal desire we find many extraordinary differences. The animal tends to eat with his stomach, and the man with his brain. When the animal's stomach is full, he stops eating, but the man is never sure when to stop. When he has eaten as much as his belly can take, he still feels empty, he still feels an urge for further gratification. This is largely due to anxiety, to the knowledge that a constant supply of food is uncertain. Therefore eat as much as you can while you can. It is due, also, to the knowledge that, in an insecure world, pleasure is uncertain. Therefore the immediate pleasure of eating must be exploited to the full, even though it does violence to the digestion.

Human desire tends to be insatiable. We are so anxious for pleasure that we can never get enough of it. We stimulate our sense organs until they become insensitive, so that if pleasure is to continue they must have stronger and stronger stimulants. In self-defense the body gets ill from the strain, but the brain wants to go on and on. The brain is in pursuit of happiness, and because the brain is much more concerned about the future than the present, it conceives happiness as the guarantee of an indefinitely long future of pleasures. Yet the brain also knows that it does not have an indefinitely long future, so that, to be happy, it must try to crowd all the pleasures of Paradise and eternity into the span of a few years.

This is why modern civilization is in almost every respect a vicious circle. It is insatiably hungry because its way of life condemns it to perpetual frustration. As we have seen, the root of this frustration is that we live for the future, and the future is an abstraction, a rational inference from experience, which exists only for the brain. The "primary consciousness," the basic mind which knows reality rather than ideas about it, does not know the future. It lives completely in the present, and perceives nothing more than what *is* at this moment. The ingenious brain, however, looks at that part of present experience called memory, and by studying it is able to make predictions. These predictions are, relatively, so accurate and reliable (e.g., "everyone will die") that the future assumes a high degree of reality—so high that the present loses its value.

But the future is still not here, and cannot become a part of experienced reality until it is present. Since what we know of the future is made up of purely abstract and logical elements—inferences, guesses, deductions—it cannot be eaten, felt, smelled, seen, heard, or otherwise enjoyed. To pursue it is to pursue a constantly retreating phantom, and the faster you chase it, the faster it runs ahead. This is why all the affairs of civilization are rushed, why hardly anyone enjoys what he has, and is forever seeking more and more. Happiness, then, will consist, not of solid and substantial realities, but of such abstract and superficial things as promises, hopes, and assurances.

Thus the "brainy" economy designed to produce this happiness is a fantastic vicious circle which must either manufacture more and more pleasures or collapse—providing a constant titillation of the ears, eyes, and nerve ends with incessant streams of almost inescapable noise and visual distractions. The perfect "subject" for the aims of this economy is the person who continuously itches his ears with the radio, preferably using the portable kind which can go with him at all hours and in all places. His eyes flit without rest from television screen, to newspaper, to magazine, keeping him in a sort of orgasm-without-release through a series of teasing glimpses of shiny automobiles, shiny female bodies, and other sensuous surfaces, interspersed with such restorers of sensitivity—shock treatments—as "human interest" shots of criminals, mangled bodies, wrecked airplanes, prize fights, and burning buildings. The literature or discourse that goes along with this is similarly manufactured to tease without satisfaction, to replace every partial gratification with a new desire.

For this stream of stimulants is designed to produce cravings for more and more of the same, though louder and faster, and these cravings drive us to do work which is of no interest save for the money it pays—to buy more lavish radios, sleeker automobiles, glossier magazines, and better television sets, all of which will somehow conspire to persuade us that happiness lies just around the corner if we will buy one more.

Despite the immense hubbub and nervous strain, we are convinced that sleep is a waste of valuable time and continue to chase these fantasies far into the night. Animals spend much of their time dozing and idling pleasantly, but, because life is short, human beings must cram into the years the highest possible amount of consciousness, alertness, and chronic insomnia so as to be sure not to miss the last fragment of startling pleasure.

It isn't that the people who submit to this kind of thing are immoral. It isn't that the people who provide it are wicked exploiters; most of them are of the same mind as the exploited, if only on a more expensive horse in this sorry-go-round. The real trouble is that they are all totally frustrated, for trying to please the brain is like trying to drink through your ears. Thus they are increasingly incapable of real pleasure, insensitive to the most acute and subtle joys of life which are in fact extremely common and simple.

The vague, nebulous, and insatiable character of brainy desire makes it particularly hard to come down to earth—to be material and real. Generally speaking, the civilized man does not know what he wants. He works for success, fame, a happy marriage, fun, to help other people, or to be a "real person." But these are not real wants because they are not actual things. They are the by-products, the flavors and atmospheres of real things—shadows which have no existence apart from some substance. Money is the perfect symbol of all such desires, being a mere symbol of real wealth, and to make it one's goal is the most blatant example of confusing measurements with reality.

It is therefore far from correct to say that modern civilization is materialistic, that is, if a materialist is a person who loves matter. The brainy modern loves not matter but measures, no solids but surfaces. He drinks for the percentage of alcohol ("spirit") and not for the "body" and taste of the liquid. He builds to put up an impressive "front" rather than to provide a space for living. Therefore he tends to put up structures which appear from the outside to be baronial mansions but are inwardly warrens. The individual living-units in these warrens are designed less for living as for creating an impression. The

main space is devoted to a "living room" of propor-
tions suitable to a large house, while such essential
spaces for living (rather than mere "entertaining")
as the kitchen are reduced to small closets where one
can hardly move—much less cook. Consequently
these wretched little galleys provide fare which is
chiefly gaseous—cocktails and "appetizers" rather
than honest meals. Because we all want to be "ladies
and gentlemen" and look as if we had servants, we
do not soil our hands with growing and cooking real
food. Instead we buy products designed for "front"
and appearance rather than content—immense and
tasteless fruit, bread which is little more than a light
froth, wine faked with chemicals, and vegetables
flavored with the arid concoctions of test tubes which
render them so much impressive pulp.

One might suppose that the most outright example
of civilized man's beastliness and animality is his
passion for sex, but in fact there is almost nothing
beastly or animal about it. Animals have sexual in-
tercourse when they feel like it, which is usually in
some sort of rhythmic pattern. Between whiles it
does not interest them. But of all pleasures sex is the
one which the civilized man pursues with the greatest anxiey. That the craving is brainy rather than
bodily is shown by the common impotence of the
male when he comes to the act, his brain pursuing
what his genes do not at the moment desire. This
confuses him hopelessly, because he simply cannot

understand *not* wanting the great delicacy of sex when it is available. He has been hankering after it for hours and days on end, but when the reality appears his body will not co-operate.

As in eating his "eyes are bigger than his stomach," so in love he judges woman by standards that are largely visual and cerebral rather than sexual and visceral. He is attracted to his partner by the surface gloss, by the film on the skin rather than the real body. He wants something with a bone structure like a boy's which is supposed to support the exterior curves and smooth undulations of femininity—not a woman but an inflated rubber dream. The function of sex itself remains, however, so much in the domain of "instinctual wisdom" that little can be done to increase its already intense pleasure, to make it faster, fancier, and more frequent. The only means of exploiting it is through cerebral fantasy, through surrounding it with coquetterie and suggestions of unspecified delights to come—as if a more ecstatic embrace could always be arranged through surface alterations.

A particularly significant example of brain against body, or measures against matter, is urban man's total slavery to clocks. A clock is a convenient device for arranging to meet a friend, or for helping people to do things together, although things of this kind happened long before they were invented. Clocks should not be smashed; they should simply be kept

in their place. And they are very much out of place
when we try to adapt our biological rhythms of eating, sleeping, evacuation, working, and relaxing to
their uniform circular rotation. Our slavery to these
mechanical drill masters has gone so far and our
whole culture is so involved with it that reform is a
forlorn hope; without them civilization would collapse entirely. A less brainy culture would learn to
synchronize its body rhythms rather than its clocks.

The capacity of the brain to foresee the future has
much to do with the fear of death. One knows of
many people who would have said with Stevenson,

> *Under the wide and starry sky*
> *Dig me a grave and let me lie;*
> *Glad did I live and gladly die,*
> *And I laid me down with a will.*

For when the body is worn out and the brain is tired,
the whole organism welcomes death. But it is difficult to understand how death can be welcome when
you are young and strong, so that you come to regard
it as a dread and terrible event. For the brain, in its
immaterial way, looks into the future and conceives
it a good to go on and on and on forever—not realizing that its own material would at last find the
process intolerably tiresome. Not taking this into account, the brain fails to see that, being itself material
and subject to change, its desires will change, and a
time will come when death will be good. On a bright

morning, after a good night's rest, you do not want to go to sleep. But after a hard day's work the sensation of dropping into unconsciousness is extraordinarily pleasant.

Unfortunately, not very many of us die peacefully. We die through accidents and painful diseases, and it is tragic indeed when a person whose "mind" is still young and alert struggles uselessly with a dying body. I am sure, however, that the body dies because it wants to. It finds it beyond its power to resist the disease or to mend the injury, and so, tired out with the struggle, turns to death. If the consciousness were more sensitive to the feelings and impulses of the whole organism, it would share this desire, and, indeed, sometimes does so. We come close to it when, in serious sickness, we would just as soon die, though sometimes we survive, either because medical treatment reinvigorates the body, or because there are still unconscious forces in the organism which are able to heal.

Accustomed, as it is, to think of man as a dualism of mind and body, and to regard the former as "sensible" and the latter as a "dumb" animal, our culture is an affront to the wisdom of nature and a ruinous exploitation of the human organism as a whole. We are perpetually frustrated because the verbal and abstract thinking of the brain gives the false impression of being able to cut loose from all finite limitations. It forgets that an infinity of anything is not a reality but an abstract concept, and persuades us that we desire this fantasy as a real goal of living.

The externalized symbol of this way of thinking is that almost entirely rational and inorganic object, the machine, which gives us the sense of being able to approach infinity. For the machine can submit to strains far beyond the capacity of the body, and to monotonous rhythms which the human being could never stand. Useful as it would be as a tool and a servant, we worship its rationality, its efficiency, and its power to abolish limitations of time and space, and thus permit it to regulate our lives. Thus the working inhabitants of a modern city are people who live inside a machine to be batted around by its wheels. They spend their days in activities which largely boil down to counting and measuring, living in a world of rationalized abstraction which has little relation to or harmony with the great biological rhythms and processes.

As a matter of fact, mental activities of this kind can now be done far more efficiently by machines than by men—so much so that in a not too distant future the human brain may be an obsolete mechanism for logical calculation. Already the human computer is widely displaced by mechanical and electrical computers of far greater speed and efficiency. If, then, man's principal asset and value is his brain and his ability to calculate, he will become an unsaleable commodity in an era when the mechanical operation of reasoning can be done more effectively by machines.[1]

Already man uses innumerable gadgets to displace the work done by bodily organs in the animals, and it would surely be in line with this tendency to externalize the reasoning functions of the brain—and thus hand over the government of life to electromagnetic monsters. In other words, the interests and goals of rationality are not those of man as a whole organism. If we are to continue to live for the future, and to make the chief work of the mind prediction and calculation, man must eventually become a parasitic appendage to a mass of clockwork.

There is, indeed, a viewpoint from which this "rationalization" of life is not rational. The brain is clever enough to see the vicious circle which it has made for itself. But it can do nothing about it. Seeing that it is unreasonable to worry does not stop worrying; rather, you worry the more at being unreason-

[1] I take my facts on this matter from Norbert Wiener's remarkable book *Cybernetics* (New York & Paris, 1948). Dr. Wiener is one of the mathematicians chiefly responsible for the development of the more elaborate electrical computers. Having likewise an advanced knowledge of neurology, he is well able to judge the extent to which these inventions can reproduce the work of the human organism. His book contains the following pertinent observation: "It is interesting to note that we may be facing one of those limitations of nature, in which highly specialized organs reach a level of declining efficiency, and ultimately lead to the extinction of the species. The human brain may be as far along on its road to this destructive specialization as the great nose horns of the last of the titanotheres." (p. 180.)

able. It is unreasonable to wage a modern war, in which everybody loses. Neither side actually wants a war, and yet, because we live in a vicious circle, we start the war to prevent the other side from starting first. We arm ourselves knowing that if we do not, the other side will—which is quite true, because if we do not arm the other side will do so to gain its advantage without actually fighting.

From this rational point of view we find ourselves in the dilemma of St. Paul—"To will is present with me; but how to perform that which is good I find not. For the good that I would I do not." But this is not, as St. Paul supposed, because the will or the "spirit" is reasonable and the flesh perverse. It is because "a house divided against itself cannot stand." The whole organism is perverse because the brain is split from the belly and the head unconscious of its union with the tail.

There are few grounds for hoping that, in any immediate future, there will be any recovery of social sanity. It would seem that the vicious circle must become yet more intolerable, more blatantly and desperately circular before any large numbers of human beings awaken to the tragic trick which they are playing on themselves. But for those who see clearly that it is a circle and why it is a circle, there is no alternative but to stop circling. For as soon as you see the whole circle, the illusion that the head is separate from the tail disappears.

And then, when experience stops oscillating and writhing, it can again become sensitive to the wisdom of the body, to the hidden depths of its own substance.

Because I speak of the wisdom of the *body* and of the necessity for recognizing that we are *material,* this is not to be taken as a philosophy of "materialism" in the accepted sense. I am not asserting that the ultimate reality *is* matter. *Matter* is a word, a noise, which refers to the forms and patterns taken by a process. We do not know *what* this process is, because it is not a "what"—that is, a thing definable by some fixed concept or measure. If we want to keep the old language, still using such terms as "spiritual" and "material," the spiritual must mean "the indefinable," that which, because it is living, must ever escape the framework of any fixed form. Matter is spirit named.

After all this, the brain deserves a word for itself! For the brain, including its reasoning and calculating centers, is a part and product of the body. It is as natural as the heart and stomach, and, rightly used, is anything but an enemy of man. But to be used rightly it must be put in its place, for the brain is made for man, not man for his brain. In other words, the function of the brain is to serve the present and the real, not to send man chasing wildly after the phantom of the future.

Furthermore, in our habitual state of mental tension the brain does not work properly, and this is one reason why its abstractions seem to have so great a reality. When the heart is out of order, we are clearly conscious of its beating; it becomes a distraction, pounding within the breast. It seems most probable that our preoccupation with thinking and planning, together with the sense of mental fatigue, is a sign of some disorder of the brain. The brain should, and in some cases does, calculate and reason with the unconscious ease of the other bodily organs. After all, the brain is not a muscle, and is thus not designed for effort and strain.

But when people try to think or concentrate, they behave as if they were trying to push their brains around. They screw up their faces, knit their brows, and approach mental problems as if they were something like heaving bricks. Yet you do not have to grind and strain to digest food, and still less to see, hear, and receive other neural impressions. The "lightning calculator" who can sum a long column of figures at a glance, the intellectual genius who can comprehend a whole page of reading in a few seconds, and the musical prodigy, such as Mozart, who seems to grasp harmony and counterpoint from babyhood, are examples of the proper use of man's most marvelous instrument.

Those of us who are not geniuses know something of the same ability. Take for example the anagram POCATELDIMC. You can work over these letters for hours, trying system after system of rearrangement in order to discover the scrambled word. Try, instead, just looking at the anagram with a relaxed mind, and in a very short space of time your brain will deliver the answer without the slightest effort.[1] We rightly mistrust the "snap" answers of strained and wandering minds, but the rapid, effortless, and almost unconscious solution of logical problems is what the brain is supposed to deliver.

Working rightly, the brain is the highest form of "instinctual wisdom." Thus it should work like the homing instinct of pigeons and the formation of the foetus in the womb—without verbalizing the process or knowing "how" it does it. The self-conscious brain, like the self-conscious heart, is a disorder, and manifests itself in the acute feeling of separation between "I" and my experience. The brain can only assume its proper behavior when consciousness is doing what it is designed for: not writhing and whirling to get out of present experience, but being effortlessly aware of it.

[1] If you don't succeed within one minute, read on! Otherwise you will begin to be annoyed either with yourself, or with me, and the consequent strain will interfere with the process.

V. ON BEING AWARE

THE QUESTION "WHAT SHALL WE DO ABOUT IT?" IS only asked by those who do not understand the problem. If a problem can be solved at all, to understand it and to know what to do about it are the same thing. On the other hand, doing something about a problem which you do not understand is like trying to clear away darkness by thrusting it aside with your hands. When light is brought, the darkness vanishes at once.

This applies particularly to the problem now before us. How are we to heal the split between "I" and "me," the brain and the body, man and nature, and bring all the vicious circles which it produces to an end? How are we to experience life as something other than a honey trap in which we are the struggling flies? How are we to find security and peace of mind in a world whose very nature is insecurity, impermanence, and unceasing change? All these questions demand a method and a course of action. At the same time, all of them show that the problem has not been understood. We do not need action—yet. We need more light.

Light, here, means awareness—to be aware of life, of experience as it is at this moment, without any judgments or ideas about it. In other words, you have to see and feel what you are experiencing as it *is,* and not as it is named. This very simple "opening of the eyes" brings about the most extraordinary transformation of understanding and living, and shows that many of our most baffling problems are pure illusion. This may sound like an over-simplification because most people imagine themselves to be fully enough aware of the present already, but we shall see that this is far from true.[1]

Because awareness is a view of reality free from ideas and judgments, it is clearly impossible to define and write down *what* it reveals. Anything which can be described is an idea, and I cannot make a positive statement about something—the real world—which is *not* an idea. I shall therefore have to be content with talking about the false impressions which awareness removes, rather than the truth which it reveals. The latter can only be symbolized with words which mean little or nothing to those without a direct under-standing of the truth in question.

What is true and positive is too real and too living to be described, and to try to describe it is like put-ting red paint on a red rose. Therefore most of what follows will have to have a rather negative quality. The truth is revealed by removing things that stand in its light, an art not unlike sculpture, in which the artist creates, not by building, but by hacking away.

[1] The word "awareness" is used in the sense given to it by J. Krishnamurti, whose writings discuss this theme with extraordinary perception.

We saw that the questions about finding security and peace of mind in an impermanent world showed that the problem had not been understood. Before going any further, it must be clear that the kind of security we are talking about is primarily spiritual and psychological. To exist at all, human beings must have a minimum livelihood in terms of food, drink, and clothing—with the understanding, however, that it cannot last indefinitely. But if the assurance of a minimum livelihood for sixty years would even begin to satisfy the heart of man, human problems would amount to very little. Indeed, the very reason why we do not have this assurance is that we want so much more than the minimum necessities.

It must be obvious, from the start, that there is a contradiction in wanting to be perfectly secure in a universe whose very nature is momentariness and fluidity. But the contradiction lies a little deeper than the mere conflict between the *desire* for security and the *fact* of change. If I want to be secure, that is, protected from the flux of life, I am wanting to be separate from life. Yet it is this very sense of separateness which makes me feel insecure. To be secure means to isolate and fortify the "I," but it is just the feeling of being an isolated "I" which makes me feel lonely and afraid. In other words, the more security I can get, the more I shall want.

To put it still more plainly: the desire for security

and the feeling of insecurity are the same thing. To hold your breath is to lose your breath. A society based on the quest for security is nothing but a breath-retention contest in which everyone is as taut as a drum and as purple as a beet.

We look for this security by fortifying and enclosing ourselves in innumerable ways. We want the protection of being "exclusive" and "special," seeking to belong to the safest church, the best nation, the highest class, the right set, and the "nice" people. These defenses lead to divisions between us, and so to more insecurity demanding more defenses. Of course it is all done in the sincere belief that we are trying to do the right things and live in the best way; but this, too, is a contradiction.

I can only think seriously of trying to live up to an ideal, to improve myself, if I am split in two pieces. There must be a good "I" who is going to improve the bad "me." "I," who has the best intentions, will go to work on wayward "me," and the tussle between the two will very much stress the difference between them. Consequently "I" will feel more separate than ever, and so merely increase the lonely and cut-off feelings which make "me" behave so badly.

We can hardly begin to consider this problem unless it is clear that the craving for security is itself a pain and a contradiction, and that the more we pursue it, the more painful it becomes. This is true in whatever form security may be conceived.

You want to be happy, to forget yourself, and yet the more you try to forget yourself, the more you remember the self you want to forget. You want to escape from pain, but the more you struggle to escape, the more you inflame the agony. You are afraid and want to be brave, but the effort to be brave is fear trying to run away from itself. You want peace of mind, but the attempt to pacify it is like trying to calm the waves with a flat-iron.

We are all familiar with this kind of vicious circle in the form of worry. We know that worrying is futile, but we go on doing it because calling it futile does not stop it. We worry because we feel unsafe, and want to be safe. Yet it is perfectly useless to say that we *should* not want to be safe. Calling a desire bad names doesn't get rid of it. What we have to discover is that there is no safety, that seeking it is painful, and that when we imagine that we have found it, we don't like it. In other words, if we can really understand what we are looking for—that safety is isolation, and what we do to ourselves when we look for it —we shall see that we do not want it at all. No one has to tell you that you *should* not hold your breath for ten minutes. You know that you can't do it, and that the attempt is most uncomfortable.

The principal thing is to understand that there *is* no safety or security. One of the worst vicious circles is the problem of the alcoholic. In very many cases he knows quite clearly that he is destroying himself, that, for him, liquor is poison, that he actually hates being drunk, and even dislikes the taste of liquor. And yet he drinks. For, dislike it as he may, the experience of not drinking is worse. It gives him the "horrors," for he stands face to face with the unveiled, basic insecurity of the world.

Herein lies the crux of the matter. To stand face to face with insecurity is still not to understand it. To understand it, you must not face it but be it. It is like the Persian story of the sage who came to the door of Heaven and knocked. From within the voice of God asked, "Who is there" and the sage answered, "It is I." "In this House," replied the voice, "there is no room for thee and me." So the sage went away, and spent many years pondering over this answer in deep meditation. Returning a second time, the voice asked the same question, and again the sage answered, "It is I." The door remained closed. After some years he returned for the third time, and, at his knocking, the voice once more demanded, "Who is there?" And the sage cried, "It is thyself!" The door was opened.

To understand that there is no security is far more than to agree with the theory that all things change, more even than to observe the transitoriness of life. The notion of security is based on the feeling that there is something within us which is permanent, something which endures through all the days and changes of life. We are struggling to make sure of the permanence, continuity, and safety of this enduring core, this center and soul of our being which we call "I." For this we think to be the real man—the thinker of our thoughts, the feeler of our feelings, and the knower of our knowledge. We do not actually understand that there is no security until we realize that this "I" does not exist.

Understanding comes through awareness. Can we, then, approach our experience—our sensations, feelings, and thoughts—quite simply, as if we had never known them before, and, without prejudice, look at what is going on? You may ask, "Which experiences, which sensations and feelings, shall we look at?" I will answer, "Which ones *can* you look at?" The answer is that you must look at the ones you have *now*.

That is surely rather obvious. But very obvious things are often overlooked. If a feeling is not present, you are not aware of it. There is no experience but present experience. What you know, what you are actually aware of, is just what is happening at this moment, and no more.

But what about memories? Surely by remembering I can also know what is past? Very well, remember something. Remember the incident of seeing a friend walking down the street. What are you aware of? You are not actually watching the veritable event of your friend walking down the street. You can't go up and shake hands with him, or get an answer to a question you forgot to ask him at the past time you are remembering. In other words, you are not look-ing at the actual past at all. You are looking at a present trace of the past.

It is like seeing the tracks of a bird on the sand. I see the present tracks. I do not, at the same time, see the bird making those tracks an hour before. The bird has flown, and I am not aware of him. From the tracks I infer that a bird was there. From memories you infer that there have been past events. But you are not aware of any past events. You know the past only in the present and as part of the present.

We are seeing, then, that our experience is alto-gether momentary. From one point of view, each moment is so elusive and so brief that we cannot even think about it before it has gone. From another point of view, this moment is always here, since we know no other moment than the present moment. It is al-ways dying, always becoming past more rapidly than imagination can conceive. Yet at the same time it is always being born, always new, emerging just as rapidly from that complete unknown which we call the future. Thinking about it almost makes you breathless.

To say that experience is momentary is really to say that experience and the present moment are the same thing. To say that this moment is always dying, or becoming past, and always being born, or coming out of the unknown, is to say the same thing of ex-perience. The experience you have just had has vanished irretrievably, and all that remains of it is a sort of wake or track in the present, which we call memory. While you can make a guess as to what experience is coming next, in actual fact you do not know. Anything might happen. But the experience which is going on now is, as it were, a newborn infant which vanishes before it can even begin to get older.

While you are watching this present experience, are you aware of *someone* watching it? Can you find, in addition to the experience itself, an experiencer? Can you, at the same time, read *this* sentence and think about yourself reading it? You will find that, to think about yourself reading it, you must for a brief second stop reading. The first experience is reading. The second experience is the thought, "I am reading." Can you find any thinker, who is thinking the thought, "I am reading?" In other words, when present experience is the thought, "I am reading," can you think about yourself thinking this thought?

Once again, you must stop thinking just, "I am reading." You pass to a third experience, which is the thought, "I am thinking that I am reading." Do not let the rapidity with which these thoughts can change deceive you into the feeling that you think them all at once.

But what has happened? Never at any time were you able to separate yourself from your present thought, or your present experience. The first present experience was reading. When you tried to think about yourself reading, the experience changed, and the next present experience was the thought "I am reading." You could not separate yourself from this experience without passing on to another. It was "ring around the rosy." When you were thinking, "I am reading this sentence" you were not reading it. In other words, in each present experience you were only aware of that experience. You were never aware of being aware. You were never able to separate the thinker from the thought, the knower from the known. All you ever found was a new thought, a new experience.

To be aware, then, is to be aware of thoughts, feelings, sensations, desires, and all other forms of experience. Never at any time are you aware of anything which is *not* experience, not a thought or feeling, but instead an experiencer, thinker, or feeler. If this is so, what makes us think that any such thing exists?

We might say, for example, that the "I" who is the thinker is this physical body and brain. But this body is in no way separate from its thoughts and sensations. When you have a sensation, say, of touch, that sensation is part of your body. While that sensation is going on, you cannot move the body away from it any more than you can walk away from a headache or from your own feet. So long as it is present, that sensation is your body and is you. You can remove the body from an uncomfortable chair, but you cannot move it from the sensation of a chair.

The notion of a separate thinker, of an "I" distinct from the experience, comes from memory and from the rapidity with which thought changes. It is like whirling a burning stick to give the illusion of a continuous circle of fire. If you imagine that memory is a direct knowledge of the past rather than a present experience, you get the illusion of knowing the past and the present at the same time. This suggests that there is something in you distinct from both the past and the present experiences. You reason, "I know this present experience, and it is different from that past experience. If I can compare the two, and notice that experience has changed, I must be something constant and apart."

But, as a matter of fact, you cannot compare this present experience with a past experience. You can only compare it with a memory of the past, *which is a part of the present experience*. When you see clearly that memory is a form of present experience, it will be obvious that trying to separate yourself from this experience is as impossible as trying to make your teeth bite themselves. There is simply experience. There is not something or someone experiencing experience! You do not feel feelings, think thoughts, or sense sensations any more than you hear hearing, see sight, or smell smelling. "I feel fine" means that a fine feeling is present. It does not mean that there is one thing called an "I" and another separate thing called a feeling, so that when you bring them together this "I" *feels* the fine feeling. There are no feelings but present feelings, and whatever feeling is present is "I." No one ever found an "I" apart from some present experience, or some experience apart from an "I"—which is only to say that the two are the same thing.

As a mere philosophical argument this is a waste of time. We are not trying to have an "intellectual discussion." We are being aware of the fact that any separate "I" who thinks thoughts and experiences experience is an illusion. To understand this is to realize that life is entirely momentary, that there is neither permanence nor security, and that there is no "I" which can be protected.

There is a Chinese story of one who came to a great sage, saying, "I have no peace of mind. Please pacify my mind." The sage answered, "Bring out your mind (your 'I') before me, and I will pacify it." "These many years," he replied, "I have sought my mind, but I cannot find it." "There," concluded the sage, "it is pacified!"

The real reason why human life can be so utterly exasperating and frustrating is not because there are facts called death, pain, fear, or hunger. The madness of the thing is that when such facts are present, we circle, buzz, writhe, and whirl, trying to get the "I" out of the experience. We pretend that we are amoebas, and try to protect ourselves from life by splitting in two. Sanity, wholeness, and integration lie in the realization that we are not divided, that man and his present experience are one, and that no separate "I" or mind can be found.

While the notion that I am separate from my experience remains, there is confusion and turmoil. Because of this, there is neither awareness nor understanding of experience, and thus no real possibility of assimilating it. To understand this moment I must not try to be divided from it; I must be aware of it with my whole being. This, like refraining from holding my breath for ten minutes, is not something I *should* do. In reality, it is the only thing I *can* do. Everything else is the insanity of attempting the impossible.

To understand music, you must listen to it. But so long as you are thinking, "*I* am listening to this music," you are not listening. To understand joy or fear, you must be wholly and undividedly aware of it. So long as you are calling it names and saying, "I am happy," or "I am afraid," you are not being aware of it. Fear, pain, sorrow, and boredom must remain problems if we do not understand them, but understanding requires a single and undivided mind. This, surely, is the meaning of that strange saying, "If thine eye be single, thy whole body shall be full of light."

YOU ARE LISTENING TO A SONG. SUDDENLY I ASK, "AT this moment, who are you?" How will you answer this question immediately and spontaneously, without stopping to find words? If the question does not shock you out of listening, you will answer by humming the song. If the question surprised you, you will answer, "At this moment, who are you?" But if you stop to think, you will try to tell me, not about this moment, but about the past. I shall get information about your name and address, your business and personal history. But I asked who you *are*, not who you *were*. For to be aware of reality, of the living present, is to discover that at each moment the experience is all. There is nothing else beside it—no experience of "you" experiencing the experience.

Even in our most apparently self-conscious moments, the "self" of which we are conscious is always some particular feeling or sensation—of muscular tensions, of warmth or cold, of pain or irritation, of breath or of pulsing blood. There is never a sensation of what senses sensations, just as there is no meaning or possibility in the notion of smelling one's nose or kissing one's own lips.

In times of happiness and pleasure, we are usually ready enough to be aware of the moment, and to let the experience be all. In such moments we "forget ourselves," and the mind makes no attempt to divide itself from itself, to be separate from experience. But with the arrival of pain, whether physical or emotional, whether actual or anticipated, the split begins and the circle goes round and round.

As soon as it becomes clear that "I" cannot possibly escape from the reality of the present, since "I" is nothing other than what I know now, this inner turmoil must stop. No possibility remains but to be aware of pain, fear, boredom, or grief in the same complete way that one is aware of pleasure. The human organism has the most wonderful powers of adaptation to both physical and psychological pain. But these can only come into full play when the pain is not being constantly restimulated by this inner effort to get away from it, to separate the "I" from the feeling. The effort creates a state of tension in which the pain thrives. But when the tension ceases, mind and body begin to absorb the pain as water reacts to a blow or cut.

There is another story of a Chinese sage who was asked, "How shall we escape the heat?"—meaning, of course, the heat of suffering. He answered, "Go right into the middle of the fire." "But how, then, shall we escape the scorching flame?" "No further pain will trouble you!" We do not need to go as far as China. The same idea comes in *The Divine Comedy*, where

Dante and Virgil find that the way out of Hell lies at its very center.

In moments of great joy we do not, as a rule, stop to think, "I am happy," or, "This is joy." Ordinarily, we do not pause to think thoughts of this kind until the joy is past its peak, or unless there is some anxiety that it will go away. At such times we are so aware of the moment that no attempt is made to compare its experience with other experiences. For this reason we do not name it, for names which are not mere exclamations are based on comparisons. "Joy" is distinguished from "sorrow" by contrast, by comparing one state of mind with the other. Had we never known joy, it would be impossible to identify sorrow as sorrow.

But in reality we cannot compare joy with sorrow. Comparison is possible only by the very rapid alternation of two states of mind, and you cannot switch back and forth between the genuine feelings of joy and sorrow as you can shift your eyes between a cat and a dog. Sorrow can only be compared with the *memory* of joy, which is not at all the same thing as joy itself.

Like words, memories never really succeed in "catching" reality. Memories are somewhat abstract, being a knowledge *about* things rather than *of* things. Memory never captures the essence, the present intensity, the concrete reality of an experience. It is, as it were, the corpse of an experience, from which the life has vanished. What we know by memory, we know only at secondhand. Memories are dead because fixed. The memory of your deceased grandmother can only repeat what your grandmother was. But the real, present grandmother could always do or say something new, and you were never absolutely sure what she would do next.

There are, then, two ways of understanding an experience. The first is to compare it with the memories of other experiences, and so to name and define it. This is to interpret it in accordance with the dead and the past. The second is to be aware of it as it is, as when, in the intensity of joy, we forget past and future, let the present be all, and thus do not even stop to think, "I am happy."

Both ways of understanding have their uses. But they correspond to the difference between knowing a thing by words and knowing it immediately. A menu is very useful, but it is no substitute for the dinner. A guidebook is an admirable tool, but it is hardly to be compared with the country it describes.

The point, then, is that when we try to understand the present by comparing it with memories, we do not understand it as deeply as when we are aware of it without comparison. This, however, is usually the way in which we approach unpleasant experiences. Instead of being aware of them as they are, we try to deal with them in terms of the past. The frightened or lonely person begins at once to think, "I'm afraid," or, "I'm so lonely."

This is, of course, an attempt to avoid the experience. We don't want to be aware of *this* present. But as we cannot get out of the present, our only escape is into memories. Here we feel on safe ground, for the past is the fixed and the known—but also, of course, the dead. Thus to try to get out of, say, fear we endeavor at once to be separate from it and to "fix" it by interpreting it in terms of memory, in terms of what is already fixed and known. In other words, we try to adapt ourselves to the mysterious present by comparing it with the (remembered) past, by naming and "identifying" it.

This would be all very well if you were trying to get away from something from which you *can* get away. It is a useful process for knowing when to come in out of the rain. But it does not tell you how to live with things from which you cannot get away, which are already part of yourself. Your body does not eliminate poisons by knowing their names. To try to control fear or depression or boredom by calling them names is to resort to superstition of trust in curses and invocations.

It is so easy to see why this does not work. Obviously, we try to know, name, and define fear in order to make it "objective," that is, separate from "I." But why are we trying to be separate from fear? Because we are afraid. In other words, fear is trying to separate itself from fear, as if one could fight fire with fire.

And this is not all. The more we accustom ourselves to understanding the present in terms of memory, the unknown by the known, the living by the dead, the more desiccated and embalmed, the more joyless and frustrated life becomes. So protected from life, man becomes a sort of mollusc encrusted in a hard shell of "tradition," so that when at last reality breaks through, as it must, the tide of pent-up fear runs wild.

If, on the other hand, you are aware of fear, you realize that, because this feeling is now yourself, escape is impossible. You see that calling it "fear" tells you little or nothing about it, for the comparison and the naming is based, not on past experience, but on memory. You have then no choice but to be aware of it with your whole being as an entirely new experience. Indeed, *every* experience is in this sense new, and at every moment of our lives we are in the midst of the new and the unknown. At this point you receive the experience without resisting it or naming it, and the whole sense of conflict between "I" and the present reality vanishes.

For most of us this conflict is ever gnawing within us because our lives are one long effort to resist the unknown, the real present in which we live, which is the unknown in the midst of coming into being. Living thus, we never really learn to live with it. At every moment we are cautious, hesitant, and on the defensive. And all to no avail, for life thrusts us into the unknown willy-nilly, and resistance is as futile and exasperating as trying to swim against a roaring torrent.

The art of living in this "predicament" is neither careless drifting on the one hand nor fearful clinging to the past and the known on the other. It consists in being completely sensitive to each moment, in regarding it as utterly new and unique, in having the mind open and wholly receptive.

This is not a philosophical theory but an experiment. One has to make the experiment to understand that it brings into play altogether new powers of adaptation to life, of literally *absorbing* pain and insecurity. It is as hard to describe how this absorption works as to explain the beating of one's heart or the formation of genes. The "open" mind does this as most of us breathe: without being able to explain it at all. The principle of the thing is clearly something like *judo,* the gentle (*ju*) way (*do*) of mastering an opposing force by giving in to it.

The natural world gives us many examples of the great effectiveness of this way. The Chinese philosophy of which *judo* itself is an expression—Taoism— drew attention to the power of water to overcome all obstacles by its gentleness and pliability. It showed how the supple willow survives the tough pine in a snowstorm, for whereas the unyielding branches of the pine accumulate snow until they crack, the springy boughs of the willow bend under its weight, drop the snow, and jump back again.

If, when swimming, you are caught in a strong current, it is fatal to resist. You must swim with it and gradually edge to the side. One who falls from a height with stiff limbs will break them, but if he relaxes like a cat he will fall safely. A building without "give" in its structure will easily collapse in storm or earthquake, and a car without the cushioning of tires and springs will soon come apart on the road.

The mind has just the same powers, for it has *give* and can *absorb* shocks like water or a cushion. But this giving way to an opposing force is not at all the same thing as running away. A body of water does not run away when you push it; it simply gives at the point of the push and encloses your hand. A shock absorber does not fall down like a bowling-pin when struck; it gives, and yet stays in the same place. To run away is the only defense of something *rigid* against an overwhelming force. Therefore the good shock absorber has not only "give," but also stability or "weight."

This weight is likewise a function of the mind, and appears in the much-misunderstood phenomenon of laziness. Significantly enough, nervous and frustrated people are always busy, even in being idle, such idleness being the "laziness" of fear, not of rest. But the mind-body is a system which conserves and accumulates energy. While doing this it is properly lazy. When the energy is stored, it is just as happy to move, and yet to move skillfully—along the line of least resistance. Thus it is not only necessity, but also laziness, which is the mother of invention. One may observe the unhurried, "heavy" movements of a skillful laborer at some hard task, and even in going against gravity the good mountaineer uses gravity, taking slow, heavy strides. He seems to tack up the slope, like a sailboat against the wind.

In the light of these principles, how does the mind absorb suffering? It discovers that resistance and escape—the "I" process—is a false move. The pain is inescapable, and resistance as a defense only makes it worse; the whole system is jarred by the shock. Seeing the impossibility of this course, it must act according to its nature—remain stable and absorb.

To remain stable is to refrain from trying to separate yourself from a pain because you know that you cannot. Running away from fear is fear, fighting pain is pain, trying to be brave is being scared. If the mind is in pain, the mind is pain. The thinker has no other form than his thought. There is no escape. But so long as you are not aware of the inseparability of thinker and thought, you will try to escape.

From this follows, quite naturally, absorption. It is no effort; the mind does it by itself. Seeing that there is no escape from the pain, the mind yields to it, absorbs it, and becomes conscious of just pain without any "I" feeling it or resisting it. It experiences pain in the same complete, unselfconscious way in which it experiences pleasure. Pain is the nature of this present moment, and I can only live in this moment.

Sometimes, when resistance ceases, the pain simply goes away or dwindles to an easily tolerable ache. At other times it remains, but the absence of any resistance brings about a way of feeling pain so unfamiliar as to be hard to describe. The pain is no longer *problematic*. I feel it, but there is no urge to get rid of it, for I have discovered that pain and the effort to be separate from it are the same thing. Wanting to get out of pain *is* the pain; it is not the "reaction" of an "I" distinct from the pain. When you discover this, the desire to escape "merges" into the pain itself and *vanishes*.

Discounting aspirin for the moment, you cannot remove your head from a headache as you can remove your hand from a flame. "You" equals "head" equals "ache." When you actually see that you *are* the pain, pain ceases to be a motive, for there is no one to be moved. It becomes, in the true sense, of no consequence. It hurts—period.

This, however, is not an experiment to be held in reserve, as a trick, for moments of crisis. It is a way of life. It means being aware, alert, and sensitive to the present moment always, in all actions and relations whatsoever, beginning at this instant. This, in turn, depends upon seeing that you have really no choice but to be aware—because you cannot separate yourself from the present and you cannot define it. You can, indeed, refuse to admit this, but only at the cost of the immense and futile effort of spending your whole life resisting the inevitable.

Once this is understood, it is really absurd to say that there is a choice or an alternative between these two ways of life, between resisting the stream in fruitless panic, and having one's eyes opened to a new world, transformed, and ever new with wonder. The key is understanding. To ask how to do this, what is the technique or method, what are the steps and rules, is to miss the point utterly. Methods are for creating things which do not yet exist. We are concerned here with understanding something which *is* —the present moment. This is not a psychological or spiritual discipline for self-improvement. It is simply being aware of this present experience, and realizing that you can neither define it nor divide yourself from it. There is no rule but "Look!"

It is no mere poetic sentiment to say that, with the mind thus opened, we look into a new world, as new as on the first day of creation "when the morning stars sang together, and all the sons of God shouted for joy." By trying to understand everything in terms of memory, the past, and words, we have, as it were, had our noses in the guidebook for most of our lives, and have never looked at the view. Whitehead's criticism of traditional education is applicable to our whole way of living:

> We are too exclusively bookish in our scholastic routine. . . . In the Garden of Eden Adam saw the animals before he named them: in the traditional system, children named the animals before they saw them.[1]

In the widest sense of the word, to name is to interpret experience by the past, to translate it into terms of memory, to bind the unknown into the system of the known. Civilized man knows of hardly any other way of understanding things. Everybody, everything, has to have its label, its number, certificate, registration, classification. What is not classified is irregular, unpredictable, and dangerous. Without passport, birth certificate, or membership in some nation, one's existence is not recognized. If you do not agree with the capitalists, they call you a communist, and *vice versa*. A person who agrees with neither point of view is fast becoming unintelligible.

That there is a way of looking at life apart from all conceptions, beliefs, opinions, and theories is the remotest of all possibilities from the modern mind. If such a point of view exists, it can only be in the vacant brain of a moron. We suffer from the delusion that the entire universe is held in order by the categories of human thought, fearing that if we do not

[1] A. N. Whitehead, *Science and the Modern World.* (Cambridge, 1933) p. 249.

hold to them with the utmost tenacity, everything will vanish into chaos.

We must repeat: memory, thought, language, and logic are essential to human life. They are one half of sanity. But a person, a society, which is only half sane is insane. To look at life without words is not to lose the ability to form words—to think, remember, and plan. To be silent is not to lose your tongue. On the contrary, it is only through silence that one can discover something new to talk about. One who talked incessantly, without stopping to look and listen, would repeat himself *ad nauseam*.

It is the same with thinking, which is really silent talking. It is not, by itself, open to the discovery of anything new, for its only novelties are simply rearrangements of old words and ideas. There was a time when language was constantly being enriched by new words—a time when men, like Adam, saw things before they named them. Today, almost all new words are rearrangements of old words, for we are no longer thinking creatively. By this I do not mean that we ought all to be popping with inventions and revolutionary discoveries. This is the—always rare—power of those who can both see the unknown and interpret it. For most of us, the other half of sanity lies simply in seeing and enjoying the unknown, just as we can enjoy music without knowing either how it is written or how the body hears it.

Certainly the revolutionary thinker must go beyond thought. He knows that almost all his best ideas come to him when thinking has stopped. He may have struggled and struggled to understand a problem in terms of old ways of thinking, only to find it impossible. But when thought stops from exhaustion, the mind is open to see the problem as it is—not as it is verbalized—and at once it is understood.

But going beyond thought is not reserved to men of genius. It is open to all of us in so far as "the mystery of life is not a problem to be solved, but a reality to be experienced." It is given to many to be seers, but to few to be prophets. Many can listen to music, but few can perform and compose. But you cannot even listen if you can hear only in terms of the past. What should we make of one of Mozart's symphonies if our ears were attuned only to the music of tom-toms? We might get the rhythms, but almost nothing of the harmony and melody. In other words, we should fail to discover an essential element of the music. To be able to hear, much less write, such a symphony men had to discover new noises— the vibrations of catgut, the sound of air in a tube, and the hum of a plucked wire. They had to discover the whole world of tone, as something entirely different from pulse.

If I can only conceive pulse, I cannot appreciate tone. If I can think of painting only as a way of making colored photographs without a camera, I can see nothing but ineptitude in a Chinese landscape. We learn nothing of very much importance when it can be explained entirely in terms of past experience. If it were possible to understand all things in terms of what we know already, we could convey the sense of color to a blind man with nothing but sound, taste, touch, and smell.

If this is true in the various arts and sciences, it is a thousand times more true when we come to the understanding of life in a larger sense and want to have some knowledge of the ultimate Reality, or God. It is surely absurd to seek God in terms of a preconceived idea of what God is. To seek thus is only to find what we know already, which is why it is so easy to deceive oneself into all manner of "supernatural" experiences and visions. To believe in God and to look for the God you believe in is simply to seek confirmation of an opinion. To ask for a revelation of God's will, and then to "test" it by reference to your preconceived moral standards is to make a mockery of asking. You knew the answer already. Seeking for "God" in this way is no more than asking for the stamp of absolute authority and certainty on what you believe in any case, for a guarantee that the unknown and the future will be a continuation of what you want to retain from the past—a bigger and better fortress for "I." *Ein feste Burg!*

If we are open only to discoveries which will accord with what we know already, we may as well stay shut. This is why the marvelous achievements of science and technology are of so little real use to us. It is in vain that we can predict and control the course of events in the future, unless we know how to live in the present. It is in vain that doctors prolong life if we spend the extra time being anxious to live still longer. It is in vain that engineers devise faster and easier means of travel if the new sights that we see are merely sorted and understood in terms of old prejudices. It is in vain that we get the power of the atom if we are just to continue in the rut of blowing people up.

Tools such as these, as well as the tools of language and thought, are of real use to men only if they are awake—not lost in the dreamland of past and future, but in the closest touch with that point of experience where reality can alone be discovered: this moment. Here life is alive, vibrant, vivid, and present, containing depths which we have hardly begun to explore. But to see and understand it at all, the mind must not be divided into "I" and "this experience." The moment must be what it always is—all that you are and all that you know. In *this* house there is no room for thee and me!

VII. THE TRANSFORMATION
OF LIFE

THE WHITE MAN FANCIES HIMSELF AS A PRACTICAL person who wants to "get results." He is impatient with theory, and with any discussion which does not immediately get down to concrete applications. This is why the behavior of Western civilization might be described, in general, as "Much Ado About Nothing." The proper meaning of "theory" is not idle speculation but *vision,* and it was rightly said that "where there is no vision the people perish."

But vision in this sense does not mean dreams and ideals for the future. It means understanding of life as it is, of what we are, and what we are doing. Without such understanding it is simply ridiculous to talk of being practical and getting results. It is like walking busily in a fog: you just go round and round. You do not know where you are going, nor what results you really want.

To minds that think in this way, what we have discussed so far may seem too theoretical. These ideas are all very well, but do they work? Yet I must ask, "What do you mean by work?" The usual "working test" of a philosophy is whether it makes people better and happier, whether it results in peace, co-operation, and prosperity. Yet this is a meaningless criterion without much "theoretical" understanding. What do you mean by happiness? What are "better" people better for? About what will you co-operate? What will you do with peace and prosperity?

The answer to these questions depends entirely on what we are and what we actually want now. If, for example, we want at the same time both peace and isolation, brotherhood and security for "I," happiness and permanence, our wants are contradictory. Their results, however practical we may be about getting them, will be further contradictions. It is the old story of wanting to have your cake and eat it—to which the only possible conclusion is that you put it in your stomach and *keep* it there until you have violent indigestion.

If we must be nationalists and have a sovereign state, we cannot also expect to have world peace. If we want to get everything at the lowest possible cost, we cannot expect to get the best possible quality, the balance between the two being mediocrity. If we make it an ideal to be morally superior, we cannot at the same time avoid self-righteousness. If we cling to belief in God, we cannot likewise have faith, since faith is not clinging but letting go.

When we have made up our minds as to what we *do* want, there remain indeed many practical and technical problems. But there is no point at all in discussing these until we have made up our minds. There is, in turn, no possibility of making up our minds so long as they are split in two, so long as "I" am one thing and "experience" another. If the mind is the directive force behind action, the mind and its vision of life must be healed before action can be anything but conflict.

Something must therefore be said about the healed vision of life which comes with full awareness, for it involves a deep transformation of our view of the world. As well as words can describe it, this transformation consists in knowing and feeling that the world is an organic unity.

In the ordinary way, we "know" this as a matter of information but do not feel it to be true. Certainly most people feel separate from everything that surrounds them. On the one hand there is myself, and on the other the rest of the universe. I am not rooted in the earth like a tree. I rattle around independently. I seem to be the center of everything, and yet cut off and alone. I can feel what is going on inside my own body, but I can only guess what is going on in others. My conscious mind must have its roots and origins in the most unfathomable depths of being, yet it feels as if it lived all by itself in this tight little skull.

Nevertheless, the physical reality is that my body exists only in relation to this universe, and in fact I am as attached to it and dependent on it as a leaf on a tree. I feel cut off only because I am split within myself, because I try to be divided from my own feelings and sensations. What I feel and sense therefore seems foreign to me. And on being aware of the unreality of this division, the universe does not seem foreign any more.

For I am what I know; what I know is I. The sensation of a house across the street or of a star in outer space is no less I than an itch on the sole of my foot or an idea in my brain. In another sense, I am also what I do not know. I am not aware of my own brain *as* a brain. In just the same way, I am not aware of the house across the street as a thing apart from my sensation of it. I know my brain as thoughts and feelings, and I know the house as sensations. In the same way and sense that I do not know my own brain, or the house as a thing-in-itself, I do not know the private thoughts in your brain.

But my brain, which is also I, your brain and the thoughts within it, as well as the house across the street, are all forms of an inextricably interwoven process called the real world. Conscious or unconscious of it as I may be, it is all I in the sense that the sun, the air, and human society are just as vital to me as my brain or my lungs. If, then, this brain is my brain—unaware of it as I am—the sun is my sun, the air my air, and society my society.

Certainly I cannot command the sun to be egg-shaped, nor force your brain to think differently. I cannot see the inside of the sun, nor can I share your private feelings. Yet neither can I change the shape or structure of my own brain, nor have a sensation of it as a contraption like a cauliflower. But if my brain is nonetheless I, the sun is I, the air is I, and society, of which you are a member, is also I—for all these things are just as essential to my existence as my brain.

That there is a sun apart from my sensation of it is an inference. The fact that I have a brain, though I cannot see it, is likewise an inference. We know about these things only in theory, and not by immediate experience. But this "external" world of theoretical objects is, apparently, just as much a unity as the "internal" world of experience. From experience I infer that it exists. And because experience is a unity—I am my sensations—I must likewise infer that this theoretical universe is a unity, that my body and the world form a single process.

Now there have been many theories about the unity of the universe. But they have not delivered human beings from the isolation of egotism, from conflict, and from the fear of life, because there is a world of difference between an inference and a feeling. You can reason that the universe is a unity without feeling it to be so. You can establish the theory that your body is a movement in an unbroken process which includes all suns and stars, and yet continue to feel separate and lonely. For the feeling will not correspond to the theory until you have also discovered the unity of inner experience. Despite all theories, you will feel that you are isolated from life so long as you are divided within.

But you will cease to feel isolated when you recognize, for example, that you do not *have* a sensation of the sky: you *are* that sensation. For all purposes of feeling, your sensation of the sky is the sky, and there is no "you" apart from what you sense, feel, and know. This is why the mystics and many of the poets give frequent utterance to the feeling that they are "one with the All," or "united with God," or, as Sir Edwin Arnold expressed it—

> *Foregoing self, the universe grows I.*

Sometimes, indeed, this feeling is purely sentimental, the poet being "one with Nature" just so long as she is on her best behavior.

> *I live not in myself, but I become*
> *Portion of that around me; and to me*
> *High mountains are a feeling, but the hum*
> *Of human cities torture: I can see*
> *Nothing to loathe in nature, save to be*
> *A link reluctant in a fleshly chain,*
> *Classed among creatures, when the soul can flee,*
> *And with the sky, the peak, the heaving plain*
> *Of ocean, or the stars, mingle, and not in vain.*

This rural rapture from Byron is quite beside the point. He has only come to terms with nature to the extent that he has befriended his own human nature.

The fly likes the sweetness of the honey, but not its stickiness, which makes him

> *A link reluctant in a fleshly chain,*
> *Classed among creatures.*

The sentimentalist does not look into the depths of nature and see

> *Sluggish existences grazing there, suspended, or slowly crawling close to the bottom: . . .*
> *The leaden-eyed shark, the walrus, the turtle, the hairy sea-leopard, and the sting-ray,*
> *Passions there, wars, pursuits, tribes—sight in those ocean depths—breathing that thick breathing air.*

Man has to discover that everything which he beholds in nature—the clammy foreign-feeling world of the ocean's depths, the wastes of ice, the reptiles of the swamp, the spiders and scorpions, the deserts of lifeless planets—has its counterpart within himself. He is not, then, at one with himself until he realizes that this "under side" of nature and the feelings of horror which it gives him are also "I."

For all the qualities which we admire or loathe in the world around us are reflections from within—though from a within that is also a beyond, unconscious, vast, unknown. Our feelings about the crawling world of the wasps' nest and the snake pit are feelings about hidden aspects of our own bodies and brains, and of all their potentialities for unfamiliar creeps and shivers, for unsightly diseases, and unimaginable pains.

I do not know whether it is true, but it is said that some of the great sages and "holy men" have an apparently supernatural power over beasts and reptiles which are always dangerous to ordinary mortals. If this is true, it is certainly because they are able to live at peace with the "beasts and reptiles" in themselves. They need not call the wild elephant Behemoth or the sea-monster Leviathan; they address them familiarly as "Long-Nose" and "Slimy."

The sense of unity with the "All" is not, however, a nebulous state of mind, a sort of trance, in which all form and distinction is abolished, as if man and the universe merged into a luminous mist of pale mauve. Just as process and form, energy and matter, myself and experience, are names for, and ways of looking at, the same thing—so one and many, unity and multiplicity, identity and difference, are not mutually exclusive opposites: they are each other, much as the body is its various organs. To discover that the many are the one, and that the one is the many, is to realize that both are words and noises representing what is at once obvious to sense and feeling, and an enigma to logic and description.

A young man in search of spiritual wisdom put himself under the instruction of a celebrated holy man. The sage made him his personal attendant, and after some months the young man complained that thus far he had received no instruction. "What do you mean!" exclaimed the holy man. "When you brought me my rice, didn't I eat it? When you brought me my tea, didn't I drink it? When you made salutations to me, didn't I return them? When have I ever neglected to give you instruction?" "I'm afraid I don't understand," said the young man, totally mystified. "When you want to see into it," answered the sage, "see into it directly. When you begin to think about it, it is altogether missed."

> Plucking chrysanthemums along the East fence;
> Gazing in silence at the southern hills;
> The birds flying home in pairs
> Through the soft mountain air of dusk—
> In these things there is a deep meaning,
> But when we are about to express it,
> We suddenly forget the words.

The meaning is not the contemplative, twilight, and, perhaps, superficially idyllic atmosphere beloved of Chinese poets. This is already expressed, and the poet does not gild the lily. He will not, like so many Western poets, turn philosopher and say that he is "one with" the flowers, the fence, the hills, and the birds. This, too, is gilding the lily, or, in his own Oriental idiom, "putting legs on a snake." For when you really understand that you are what you see and know, you do not run around the countryside thinking, "I *am* all this." There is simply "all this."

The feeling that we stand face-to-face with the

world, cut off and set apart, has the greatest influence on thought and action. Philosophers, for example, often fail to recognize that their remarks about the universe apply also to themselves and their remarks. If the universe is meaningless, so is the statement that it is so. If this world is a vicious trap, so is its accuser, and the pot is calling the kettle black.

In the strictest sense, we cannot actually think about life and reality at all, because this would have to include thinking about thinking, thinking about thinking about thinking, and so *ad infinitum*. One can only attempt a rational, descriptive philosophy of the universe on the assumption that one is totally separate from it. But if you and your thoughts are part of this universe, you cannot stand outside them to describe them. This is why all philosophical and theological systems must ultimately fall apart. To "know" reality you cannot stand outside it and define it; you must enter into it, be it, and feel it.

Speculative philosophy, as we know it in the West, is almost entirely a symptom of the divided mind, of man trying to stand outside himself and his experience in order to verbalize and define it. It is a vicious circle, like everything else which the divided mind attempts.

On the other hand, the realization that the mind is actually undivided must have a corresponding and equally far-reaching influence on thought and action.

As the philosopher tries to stand outside himself and his thought, so, as we have seen, the ordinary man tries to stand outside himself and his emotions and sensations, his feelings and desires. The result is a fantastic confusion and misdirection of conduct which discovery of the mind's unity must bring to an end.

So long as the mind is split, life is perpetual conflict, tension, frustration, and disillusion. Suffering is piled on suffering, fear on fear, and boredom on boredom. The more the fly struggles to get out of the honey, the faster he is stuck. Under the pressure of so much strain and futility, it is no wonder at all that men seek release in violence and sensationalism, and in the reckless exploitation of their bodies, their appetites, the material world, and their fellow men. What this must add to the necessary and unavoidable pains of existence is incalculable.

But the undivided mind is free from this tension of trying always to stand outside oneself and to be elsewhere than here and now. Each moment is lived completely, and there is thus a sense of fulfillment and completeness. The divided mind comes to the dinner table and pecks at one dish after another, rushing on without digesting anything to find one better than the last. It finds nothing good, because there is nothing which it really tastes.

When, on the other hand, you realize that you

live in, that indeed you *are* this moment now, and no other, that apart from this there is no past and no future, you must relax and taste to the full, whether it be pleasure or pain. At once it becomes obvious why this universe exists, why conscious beings have been produced, why sensitive organs, why space, time, and change. The whole problem of justifying nature, of trying to make life mean something in terms of its future, disappears utterly. Obviously, it all exists for this moment. It is a dance, and when you are dancing you are not intent on getting somewhere. You go round and round, but not under the illusion that you are pursuing something, or fleeing from the jaws of hell.

How long have the planets been circling the sun? Are they getting anywhere, and do they go faster and faster in order to arrive? How often has the spring returned to the earth? Does it come faster and fancier every year, to be sure to be better than last spring, and to hurry on its way to the spring that shall outspring all springs?

The meaning and purpose of dancing is the dance. Like music, also, it is fulfilled in each moment of its course. You do not play a sonata *in order* to reach the final chord, and if the meanings of things were simply in ends, composers would write nothing but finales. It might, however, be observed in passing that the music specially characteristic of our culture is progressive in some respects, and does at times seem to be decidedly on its way to a future climax. But when it gets there, it does not know what to do with itself. Beethoven, Brahms, and Wagner were particularly guilty of working up to colossal climaxes and conclusions, and then blasting away at the same chord over and over again, ruining the moment by being reluctant to leave it.

When each moment becomes an expectation life is deprived of fulfillment, and death is dreaded for it seems that here expectation must come to an end. While there is life there is hope—and if one lives on hope, death is indeed the end. But to the undivided mind, death is another moment, complete like every moment, and cannot yield its secret unless lived to the full—

And I laid me down with a will.

Death is the epitome of the truth that in each moment we are thrust into the unknown. Here all clinging to security is compelled to cease, and wherever the past is dropped away and safety abandoned, life is renewed. Death is the unknown in which all of us lived before birth.

Nothing is more creative than death, since it is the whole secret of life. It means that the past must be abandoned, that the unknown cannot be avoided, that "I" cannot continue, and that nothing can be ultimately fixed. When a man knows this, he lives for the first time in his life. By holding his breath, he loses it. By letting it go he finds it.

> Und so lang du das nicht hast,
> Dieses: stirb und werde,
> Bist du nur ein trüber Gast
> Auf der dunklen Erde.[1]

---

[1] Goethe, *West-östlicher Divan*. "As long as you do not know how to die and come to life again, you are but a sorry traveler on this dark earth."

VIII. CREATIVE MORALITY

IT IS PERHAPS A PARADOX TO TALK ABOUT CREATIVE morality. For "morality" is derived from a word meaning custom and convention, and the regulation of life by rules. But morality has also come to mean the working of love in human relations, and in this sense we can speak of a morality which is creative. St. Augustine described it as, "Love, and do what you will." But the problem has always been how to love what you do not like.

If morality is the art of living together, it is clear that rules, or rather techniques, have a place in it. For many of the problems of a community are technical problems—the distribution of wealth and population, the proper management of natural resources, the organization of family life, the care of the sick and disabled, and the harmonious adaptation of individual differences.

The moralist is therefore a technician who is consulted on these problems as one consults an architect on building a house or an engineer on erecting a bridge. Like medicine, shoe-making, cookery, tailoring, farming, and carpentry, living together requires a certain "know-how." It demands the acquisition and use of certain skills.

But the moralist has, in practice, become much

more than a technical consultant. He has become a scold. From his pulpit or his study he harangues the human race, issuing praise and blame—mostly blame —like fire from the mouth of a dragon. For people do not take his advice. They ask how it is best to act under such-and-such circumstances. He tells them, and they seem to agree that he is right. But then they go away and do something different, for they find his advice too difficult or have a strong desire to do the opposite. This happens so regularly that the moralist loses his temper and begins to call them bad names. When this has no effect, he resorts to physical violence, implementing his advice with policemen, punishments, and prisons. For the community is its own moralist. It elects and pays judges, policemen, and preachers, as if to say, "When I am difficult, please kick me."

At first sight the problem seems to boil down to this: Morals are for avoiding an unfair distribution of pleasure and pain. This means that some individuals must get less pleasure and more pain. As a rule, these individuals will only submit to the sacrifice under the threat of still more pain if they do not co-operate. This is based on the assumption that every man is for himself, and observes the interests of the community only to the extent that these are obviously his own interests.

From this, moralists have evolved the theory that man is basically selfish, or that he has an inherent bias towards evil. The "natural" man lives for one motive: to protect his body from pain and to associate it with pleasure. Because he can only feel with his own body, he has little interest in the feelings of other bodies. Therefore he will only take interest in other bodies under the stimulus of rewards and punishments, that is, by an exploitation of his self-interest in the interest of the community.

Happily, the problem is not quite so simple. For among the things that give man pleasure are relations with other human beings—conversation, eating together, singing, dancing, having children, and cooperation in work which "many hands make light." Indeed, one of the highest pleasures is to be more or less unconscious of one's own existence, to be absorbed in interesting sights, sounds, places, and people. Conversely, one of the greatest pains is to be self-conscious, to feel unabsorbed and cut off from the community and the surrounding world.

But this whole problem has no solution while we think about it in terms of the pleasure-pain motivation, or, indeed, in terms of any "motivation" at all. For man has a moral problem, which other community-living animals do not have, for the very reason that he is so much concerned with motives. If it is true that man is necessarily motivated by the pleasure-pain principle, there is no point whatsoever in discussing human conduct. Motivated conduct is determined conduct; it will be what it will be, no matter what anyone has to say about it. There can be no creative morality unless man has the possibility of freedom.

This is where the moralists make their mistake. If they want man to change his way of life, they must assume that he is free, for if he is not, all the raging and protesting in the world will make no difference. On the other hand, a man who is acting from the fear of a moralist's threats or from the lure of his promises is not making a free act! If man is not free, threats and promises may modify his conduct, but they will not change it in any essential respect. If he is free, threats and promises will not make him use his freedom.

The meaning of freedom can never be grasped by the divided mind. If I feel separate from my experience, and from the world, freedom will seem to be the extent to which I can push the world around, and fate the extent to which the world pushes me around. But to the whole mind there is no contrast of "I" and the world. There is just one process acting, and it does everything that happens. It raises my little finger and it creates earthquakes. Or, if you want to put it that way, *I* raise my little finger and also make earthquakes. No one fates and no one is being fated.

Of course this is a strange view of freedom. We are accustomed to think that, if there is any freedom at all, it resides, not in nature, but in the separate human will and its power of choice.

But what we ordinarily mean by choice is not freedom. Choices are usually decisions motivated by pleasure and pain, and the divided mind acts with the sole purpose of getting "I" into pleasure and out of pain. But the best pleasures are those for which we do not plan, and the worst part of pain is expecting it and trying to get away from it when it has come. You cannot plan to be happy. You can plan to exist, but in themselves existence and non-existence are neither pleasurable nor painful. I am even assured by doctors that there are circumstances under which death can be a highly pleasant experience.

The sense of not being free comes from trying to do things which are impossible and even meaningless. You are not "free" to draw a square circle, to live without a head, or to stop certain reflex actions. These are not obstacles to freedom; they are the conditions of freedom. I am not free to draw a circle if perchance it should turn out to be a square circle. I am not, thank heaven, free to walk out of doors and leave my head at home. Likewise I am not free to live in any moment but this one, or to separate myself from my feelings. In short I am not free when I am trying to do something contradictory, such as to move without changing position, or to burn my finger without feeling pain.

On the other hand, I am free, the world process is free, to do anything which is not a contradiction. The question then arises: is it a contradiction, is it impossible, to act or to decide without pleasure as the ultimate aim? The theory that we must inevitably do what gives us the greater pleasure or the lesser pain, is a meaningless assertion based on verbal confusion. To say that I decide to do something because it pleases me says only that I decide to do it because I decide to do it. If "pleasure" is defined in the beginning as "what I prefer," then what I prefer will always be pleasure. If I prefer pain, like a masochist, then pain will be pleasure. In short, the theory begs the question at the start by saying that pleasure means what we desire: therefore anything that we desire is pleasure.

But I fall straight into contradiction when I try to act and decide in order to be happy, when I make "being pleased" my future goal. For the more my actions are directed towards future pleasures, the more I am incapable of enjoying any pleasures at all. For all pleasures are present, and nothing save complete awareness of the present can even begin to guarantee future happiness. I can act in order to eat tomorrow, or take a trip to the mountains next week, but there is really no way of being certain that this will make me happy. On the contrary, it is common experience that nothing ruins a "pleasure" so much as watching yourself in the midst of it to see whether it pleases you. You can only live in one moment at a time, and you cannot think simultaneously about listening to the waves and whether you are enjoying listening to the waves. Contradictions of this kind are the only real types of action without freedom.

There is another theory of determinism which states that all our actions are motivated by "unconscious mental mechanisms," and that for this reason even the most spontaneous decisions are not free. This is but another example of split-mindedness, for what is the difference between "me" and "mental mechanisms" whether conscious or unconscious? *Who* is being moved by these processes? The notion that anyone is being motivated comes from the persisting illusion of "I." The real man, the organism-in-relation-to-the-universe, *is* this unconscious motivation. And because he *is* it, he is not being moved *by* it. In other words, it is not motivation; it is simply operation. Moreover, there is no "unconscious" mind distinct from the conscious, for the "unconscious" mind is conscious, though not of itself, just as the eyes see but do not see themselves.

There remains the supposition that the whole operation, the whole process of action which is man-and-universe, is a determined series of events in which every event is the inevitable result of past causes.

We cannot go into this problem exhaustively or even adequately. But it is perhaps enough to realize for the moment that this is one of the biggest "open questions" of science, which is far from reaching a decision. The idea that the past determines the present can be an illusion of language. Because we must describe the present in terms of the past, it would seem that the past "explains" the present. To say "how" something happened, we describe the chain of events of which it seemed to be a part.

The bottle smashed. It fell to the floor. I let it go. My fingers were slippery. I had soap on my hands. Is it legitimate to put the word "because" between these statements? We do so as a rule, for we can make the safe bet that if I let go of the bottle, it will fall to the floor. But this does not prove that I caused it to fall, or that it *must* have fallen. Events look inevitable in retrospect because when they have happened, nothing can change them. Yet the fact that I can make safe bets could prove equally well that events are not *determined* but *consistent*. In other words, the universal process acts freely and spontaneously at every moment, but tends to throw out events in regular, and so predictable, sequences.

However this issue may be decided, the undivided mind certainly has the feeling of freedom, and certainly brings into the moral sphere a way of life which has all the marks of free and creative action.

It is easy to see that most of the acts which, in conventional morals, are called evil can be traced to the divided mind. By far the greater part of these acts come from exaggerated desires, desires for things which are not even remotely necessary for the health of mind and body, granting that "health" is a relative term. Such outlandish and insatiable desires come into being because man is exploiting his appetites to give the "I" a sense of security.

I am depressed, and want to get "I" out of this depression. The opposite of depression is elation, but because depression is not elation, I cannot force myself to be elated. I can, however, get drunk. This makes me wonderfully elated, and so when the next depression arrives, I have a quick cure. The subsequent depressions have a way of getting deeper and blacker, because I am not digesting the depressed state and eliminating its poisons. So I need to get even drunker to drown them. Very soon I begin to hate myself for getting so drunk, which makes me still more depressed—and so it goes.

Or perhaps I have a large family, and am living in a mortgaged house on which I have spent all my savings. I have to work hard at a job in which I am not particularly interested in order to pay the bills. I don't mind working so much, but I keep wondering what will happen if I get sick, or if a war comes and I am drafted. I would rather not think about these things, so I want to get "I" out of this worry. For I am sure that I *shall* get sick if it goes on. But it's so hard to stop, and as this makes sickness more certain, the worrying digs deeper. I *must* find relief from this, and so in desperation I begin to "play the ponies," trying to offset the worry with the daily hope that my horse may win. And so *it* goes.

The conventional moralist has nothing to contribute to these problems. He can point out the frightful effects of alcoholism and gambling, but that is simply more fuel for depression and worry. He can promise rewards in heaven for suffering patiently endured, but that, too, is a gamble of a kind. He can attribute the depression or the worry to the social system, and urge the unfortunates to join the revolution.

In short, he can either frighten the "I" or encourage it, in one case making the individual run away from himself, and in the other making him run after himself. He can paint glowing pictures of the virtues and encourage others to find strength in the examples of great men. He can succeed to the extent of arousing the most vigorous efforts to imitate saintliness, to curb the passions, and to practice restraint and charity in action. Yet none of this brings anyone to freedom, for behind all the imitation and the discipline there is still motive.

If I am afraid, my efforts to feel and act bravely are moved by the fear, for I am afraid of fear, which is simply to say that my efforts to escape from what I am are moving in a circle. Beside the examples of saints and heroes I feel ashamed that I amount to nothing, and so I begin to practice humility because of my wounded pride, and charity because of my self-love. The urge is ever to make "I" amount to something. I must be right, good, a real person, heroic, loving, self-effacing. I efface myself in order to assert myself, and give myself away in order to keep myself. The whole thing is a contradiction.

The Christian mind has always been haunted by the feeling that the sins of the saints are worse than the sins of the sinners, that in some mysterious way the one who is struggling for salvation is nearer to hell and to the heart of evil than the unashamed harlot or thief. It has recognized that the Devil is an angel, and as pure spirit is not really interested in the sins of the flesh. The sins after the Devil's heart are the intricacies of spiritual pride, the mazes of self-deception, and the subtle mockeries of hypocrisy where mask hides behind mask behind mask and reality is lost altogether.

The would-be saint walks straight into the meshes of this web because *he* would become a saint. His "I" finds the deepest security in a satisfaction which is the more intense for being so cleverly hidden—the satisfaction of being contrite for his sins, and contrite for taking pride in his contrition. In such an involved vicious circle the masks behind masks are infinite. Or, to put it in another way, he who would stand outside himself to kick himself, must then kick the self that stands outside. And so forever.

So long as there is the motive to become some-

THE WISDOM OF INSECURITY

thing, so long as the mind believes in the possibility of escape from what it is at this moment, there can be no freedom. Virtue will be pursued for exactly the same reason as vice, and good and evil will alternate as the opposite poles of a single circle. The "saint" who appears to have conquered his self-love by spiritual violence has only concealed it. His apparent success convinces others that he has found the "true way," and they follow his example long enough for the course to swing to its opposite pole, when license becomes the inevitable reaction to puritanism.

Of course it *sounds* as if it were the most abject fatalism to have to admit that I am what I am, and that no escape or division is possible. It seems that if I *am* afraid, then I am "stuck" with fear. But in fact I am chained to the fear only so long as I am trying to get away from it. On the other hand, when I do not try to get away I discover that there is nothing "stuck" or fixed about the reality of the moment. When I am aware of this feeling without naming it, without calling it "fear," "bad," "negative," etc., it changes instantly into something else, and life moves freely ahead. The feeling no longer perpetuates itself by creating the feeler behind it.

We can perhaps see now why the undivided mind is not moved into those escapes from the present which are usually called "evil." The further truth that the undivided mind is aware of experience as a unity, of the world as itself, and that the whole nature of mind and awareness is to be one with what it knows, suggests a state that would usually be called love. For the love that expresses itself in creative action is something much more than an emotion. It is not something which *you* can "feel" and "know," remember and define. Love is the organizing and unifying principle which makes the world a *universe* and the disintegrated mass a community. It is the very essence and character of mind, and becomes manifest in action when the mind is whole.

For the mind *must* be interested or absorbed in something, just as a mirror must always be reflecting something. When it is not trying to be interested in itself—as if a mirror would reflect itself—it must be interested, or absorbed, in other people and things. There is no problem of how to love. We love. We are love, and the only problem is the direction of love, whether it is to go straight out like sunlight, or to try to turn back on itself like a "candle under a bushel."

Released from the circle of attempted self-love, the mind of man draws the whole universe into its own unity as a single dewdrop seems to contain the entire sky. This, rather than any mere emotion, is the power and principle of free action and creative morality. On the other hand, the morality of rules and regulations based on rewards and punishments, even when these are as intangible as the pain of guilt and the pleasure of self-respect, has no relation to free action. It is a way of ruling slaves by "benevolent exploitation" of their illusions, and, however far pursued, can never lead to freedom.

Where there is to be creative action, it is quite beside the point to discuss what we should or should not do in order to be right or good. A mind that is single and sincere is not interested in being good, in conducting relations with other people so as to live up to a rule. Nor, on the other hand, is it interested in being free, in acting perversely just to prove its independence. Its interest is not in itself, but in the people and problems of which it is aware; these are "itself." It acts, not according to the rules, but according to the circumstances of the moment, and the "well" it wishes to others is not security but liberty.

Nothing is really more inhuman than human relations based on morals. When a man gives bread in order to be charitable, lives with a woman in order to be faithful, eats with a Negro in order to be unprejudiced, and refuses to kill in order to be peaceful, he is as cold as a clam. He does not actually see the other person. Only a little less chilly is the benevolence springing from pity, which acts to remove suffering because it finds the sight of it disgusting.

But there is no formula for generating the authentic warmth of love. It cannot be copied. You cannot talk yourself into it or rouse it by straining at the emotions or by dedicating yourself solemnly to the service of mankind. Everyone has love, but it can only come out when he is convinced of the impossibility and the frustration of trying to love himself. This conviction will not come through condemnations, through hating oneself, through calling self-love all the bad names in the universe. It comes only in the awareness that one has no self to love.

IX. RELIGION REVIEWED

WE BEGAN THIS BOOK WITH THE ASSUMPTION THAT science and scientific philosophy give no grounds for religious belief. We did not argue the point, but took it as the point of departure. We adopted the prevalent view that the existence of God, of any absolutes, and of an eternal order beyond this world is without logical support or meaning. We accepted the notion that such ideas are of no value for scientific prediction, and that all known events can be explained more simply without them. At the same time, we said that religion had no need to oppose this view, for almost all the spiritual traditions recognize that there is a stage in man's development when belief—in contrast to faith—and its securities have to be left behind.

To this point, I do not think that we have claimed anything which cannot be verified by experiment, or asserted anything which seriously conflicts with a scientific view of the world. Yet we have now come to a position from which the principal ideas of religion and traditional metaphysics can once more become intelligible and meaningful—not as beliefs, but as valid symbols of experience.

Science and religion are talking about the same universe, but they are using different kinds of language. In general, the statements of science have to do with the past and the future. The scientist describes events. He tells us "how" things happen by giving us a detailed account of *what* has happened. He finds that events occur in various frequencies and orders, and on this basis he makes bets or predictions in the light of which we can make practical arrangements and adaptations to the course of events. To make these bets, he does not need to know about God or eternal life. He needs to know the past— what has happened already.

On the other hand, the statements of religion have to do with the present. But both religious and scientific people are under the impression that religion is more concerned with the past and the future. This is a natural misunderstanding, because religion seems to make assertions about how this world began and how it will end. It has long been connected with prophecy, which is surely the same thing as prediction. It states that this world *was made* by God, and that he made it for a *purpose* which *will be* fulfilled in the distant future, in "the life of the world to come." It insists, furthermore, that man has an immortal soul, and prophesies that it *will* survive his physical death and live everlastingly.

The scientist therefore seems justified in saying that such predictions cannot be verified, and that they are made with precious little reference to past events known to have happened. When he tries to discover the grounds upon which these predictions are made, he finds them emotional rather than rational. Religious people *hope* or believe that these things will be true.

Nevertheless, in the history of every important religion there have been those who understood religious ideas and statements in a very different way. On the whole, this has been more true of the East than of the West, though Christian history contains a long list of men and women who could have talked on common ground with orthodox Hindus and Buddhists.

From this other and, we think, deeper point of view, religion is not a system of predictions. Its doctrines have to do, not with the future and the everlasting, but with the present and the eternal. They are not a set of beliefs and hopes but, on the contrary, a set of graphic symbols about present experience.

Traditionally, these symbols are of two kinds. One describes the religious way of understanding the present in the form of concrete images and stories. The other describes it in an abstract, negative language which is often similar to the language of academic philosophy. For convenience, we can call these two kinds of symbol the religious and the metaphysical. But we must remember that "metaphysic" in this sense is not speculative philosophy. It is not an attempt to anticipate science and give a logical description of the universe and its origins. It is a way of representing a knowledge of the present. Religious symbols are specially characteristic of Christianity, Islam, and Judaism, whereas doctrines of the Oriental type are more metaphysical.

We said that science and religion are both talking about the same world, and throughout this book we have never been concerned with anything but everyday life, with things which can be seen, felt, and experienced. We shall therefore be told, by religious critics, that we are reducing religion to "naturalism," that we are identifying God with nature, and making a mockery and travesty of religion by taking away "its essential supernatural content."

But when you ask theologians what they mean by the "supernatural," they burst immediately into scientific language. They talk about a God having "concrete reality distinct from this universe," and speak of him in terms of past history and future predictions. They insist that the supernatural world is not of the same "order" as the universe studied by science, but exists on another plane of being invisible to our natural senses. It begins to sound like something psychic, something of the same order as the phenomena of telepathy, clairvoyance, and clairaudience.

Yet this is naturalism pure and simple; it is even pseudo-science. For science and naturalism are not necessarily concerned only with things visible to the senses. No one has seen electrons or quanta, nor been able to construct a sensual image of curved space. If psychic phenomena exist, there is no reason to suppose that they cannot be studied scientifically, and that they are not simply another aspect of "nature." Indeed, science is concerned with innumerable things which cannot be experienced with the senses, and which are not present to immediate experience —for example, the entire past, the process of gravity, the nature of time, and the weights of planets and stars. These invisible things are inferred from immediate experience by logic. They are hypotheses which seem to give a reasonable explanation of observed events. The theological God is exactly the same thing—a hypothesis accounting for all experiences.

When a theologian makes such a hypothesis he uses the methods of science and enters the field of science. He must expect, therefore, to be questioned, examined, and criticized by his fellow naturalists.

But the difference between the natural and the supernatural can be understood in a simpler and much more useful way. If "nature" is the province of science, we can say that nature is this world as it is named, measured, and classified. Nature is the world which thought has analyzed and sorted into groups called "things." It has, as we saw, given things an identity by naming them. It distinguishes motion from stillness by comparing something which moves rapidly in relation to something which moves slowly, though both move.

Thus the whole world of nature is relative and is produced by thought and comparison. Is the head "really" distinct from the neck? Why shouldn't we have made the "thing" called head include the "thing" called neck, just as it includes the nose? It is a convention of thought that head and neck are two things instead of one. In this sense, the ancient metaphysicians are perfectly right when they say that the whole universe is a product of the mind. They mean the universe of "things."

On the other hand, the supernatural and absolute world consists of the mysterious reality which we have so named, classified, and divided. This is not a product of the mind. But there is no way of defining or describing *what* it is. At every moment we are aware of it, and it is our awareness. We feel and sense it, and it is our feelings and sensations. Yet trying to know and define it is like trying to make a knife cut itself. What is this? This is a rose. But "a rose" is a noise. What is a noise? A noise is an impact of air waves on the eardrum. Then a rose is an impact of air waves on the eardrum? No, a rose is a rose . . . is a rose is a rose is a rose. . . .

Definition is simply making a one-to-one correspondence between groups of sense data and noises, but because noises are sense data, the attempt is ultimately circular. The real world which both provides these data and the organs wherewith to sense them remains unfathomably mysterious.

From this point of view we need have no difficulty in making sense of some of the ancient scriptures. The *Dhammapada,* a collection of sayings of the Buddha, begins: "All that we are is the result of what we have thought. It is founded on our thoughts; it is made up of our thoughts." This is, in effect, the same statement that opens St. John's Gospel: "In the beginning was the Word, and the Word was with God, and the Word was God. . . . All things were made by him (the Word), and without him was not anything made that was made." By thoughts, or mental words, we distinguish or "make" things. Without thoughts, there are no "things"; there is just undefined reality.

If you want to be poetic, you can liken this undefined reality to the Father, because it is the origin or basis of "things." You can call thought the Son "of one substance with the Father"—the Son "by whom all things were made," the Son who must be crucified if we are to see the Father, just as we must look at reality without words to see it as it is. Thereafter the Son rises from the dead and returns to heaven, and, likewise, when we see reality as it is we are free to use thought without being fooled by it. It "returns to heaven" in the sense that we recognize it as part of reality, and not something standing outside it.

Otherwise, we can use the negative, metaphysical language about this undefined reality. It is the infinite, not the definite. It is the eternal, the ever-present, not the past and future, not the conventions of thought and time. It is the unchanging in the sense that the idea of change is but another word, another definition, which the reality *called* change surpasses. Obviously, if all movement is relative, there is no absolute movement. It would be meaningless to say that *all* bodies in the universe are moving uniformly at ten thousand miles per minute, because "all" has excluded any other body with respect to which they could be said to move.

Metaphysical language is negative because it is trying to say that words and ideas do not explain reality. It is not trying to persuade us that reality is something like a boundless mass of transparent jelly. It does not speak of some impalpable abstraction, but of this very world in which we live. This experience which we call things, colors, sounds, smells, tastes, forms, and weights is, in itself, no thing, no form, no number, no nothing—but at this moment we behold it. We are, then, beholding the God which traditional doctrines call the boundless, formless, infinite, eternal, undivided, unmoved, and unchanging Reality—the Absolute behind the relative, the Meaning behind thoughts and words.[1] Naturally

[1] This is likewise what Vedanta doctrine terms the Self, the *atman,* transcending all experienced "things."

142

the Meaning is meaning-less because, unlike words, it does not *have* meaning but *is* meaning. By itself, a tree is meaningless, but it is the meaning of the word "tree."

It is easy to see that this kind of language, whether in its religious or metaphysical forms, can lead to all manner of misunderstanding. For when the mind is divided, and "I" wants to get away from present experience, the whole notion of a supernatural world is its happy hide-out. The "I" is resisting an unhappy change, and so clings to the "unchanging" Absolute, forgetting that this Absolute is also the "unfixed." When life provides some bitter experience, the "I" can only support it with the guarantee that it is part of the plan of a loving Father-God. But this very guarantee makes it impossible to realize the "love of God," which, as is well known, requires the giving up of "I."

The misunderstanding of religious ideas is vividly illustrated in what men have made of the doctrine of immortality, heaven, and hell. But now it should be clear that eternal life is the realization that the present is the only reality, and that past and future can be distinguished from it in a conventional sense alone. The moment is the "door of heaven," the "straight and narrow way that leadeth unto life," because there is no room in it for the separate "I." In *this* experience there is no one experiencing the experience. The "rich man" cannot get through this door because he carries too much baggage; he is clinging to the past and the future.

One might quote whole pages from the spiritual literature of all times and places to show that eternal life has been understood in this sense. The following from Eckhart will suffice:

> The Now-moment in which God made the first man and the Now-moment in which the last man will disappear, and the Now-moment in which I am speaking are all one in God, in whom there is only one Now. Look! The person who lives in the light of God is conscious neither of time past nor of time to come but only of one eternity. . . . Therefore he gets nothing new out of future events, nor from chance, for he lives in the Now-moment that is, unfailingly, "in verdure newly clad."

When you are dying and coming to life in each moment, would-be scientific predictions about what will happen after death are of little consequence. The whole glory of it is that we do not know. Ideas of survival and annihilation are alike based on the past, on memories of waking and sleeping, and, in their different ways, the notions of everlasting continuity and everlasting nothingness are without meaning.

It needs but slight imagination to realize that everlasting time is a monstrous nightmare, so that between heaven and hell as ordinarily understood there is little to choose. The desire to continue always can only seem attractive when one thinks of indefinite time rather than infinite time. It is one thing to have as much time as you want, but quite another to have time without end.

For there is no joy in continuity, in the perpetual. We desire it only because the present is empty. A person who is trying to eat money is always hungry. When someone says, "Time to stop now!" he is in a panic because he has had nothing to eat yet, and wants more and more time to go on eating money, ever hopeful of satisfaction around the corner. We do not really want continuity, but rather a present experience of total happiness. The thought of wanting such an experience to go on and on is the result of being self-conscious in the experience, and thus incompletely aware of it. So long as there is the feeling of an "I" *having* this experience, the moment is not *all*. Eternal life is realized when the last trace of difference between "I" and "now" has vanished—when there is just this "now" and nothing else.

By contrast, hell or "everlasting damnation" is not the everlastingness of time going on forever, but of the unbroken circle, the continuity and frustration of going round and round in pursuit of something which can never be attained. Hell is the fatuity, the everlasting impossibility, of self-love, self-consciousness, and self-possession. It is trying to see one's own eyes, hear one's own ears, and kiss one's own lips.

To see, however, that life is complete in each moment—whole, undivided, and ever new—is to understand the sense of the doctrine that in eternal life

God, the undefinable *this,* is all-in-all and is the Final Cause or End for which everything exists. Because the future is everlastingly unattainable, and, like the dangled carrot, *always* ahead of the donkey, the fulfillment of the divine purpose does not lie in the future. It is found in the present, not by an act of resignation to immovable fact, but in seeing that there is no one to resign.

For this is the meaning of that universal and ever-repeated religious principle that to know God, man must give up himself. It is as familiar as any platitude, and yet nothing has been harder to do, and nothing so totally misunderstood. How can a self, which is selfish, give itself up? Not, say the theologians, by its own power, but through the gift of divine grace, the power which enables man to achieve what is beyond his own strength. But is this grace given to all or to a chosen few, who, when they receive it, have no choice but to surrender themselves? Some say that it comes to all, but that there are those who accept its aid and those who refuse. Others say that it comes to a chosen elect, but still, for the most part, insist that the individual has the power to take it or leave it.

But this does not solve the problem at all. It replaces the problem of holding or surrendering the self by the problem of accepting or refusing divine grace, and the two problems are identical. The Chris-

tian religion contains its own hidden anwer to the
problem in the idea that man can only surrender
himself "in Christ." For "Christ" stands for the reality that there is no separate self to surrender. To give
up "I" is a false problem. "Christ" is the realization
that there is no separate "I." "I do nothing of myself.
. . . I and the Father are one. . . . Before Abra-
ham was, I am."

If there is any problem at all, it is to see that in
this instant you have no "I" to surrender. You are
completely free to do this at any moment, and nothing whatever is stopping you. This is our freedom.
We are not, however, free to improve ourselves, to
surrender ourselves, to lay ourselves open to grace,
for all such split-mindedness is the denial and post-
ponement of our freedom. It is trying to eat your
mouth instead of bread.

Is it necessary to underline the vast difference between the realization that "I and the Father are one,"
and the state of mind of the person who, as we say,
"thinks he is God"? If, still thinking that there is an
isolated "I," you identify it with God, you become
the insufferable ego-maniac who thinks himself successful in attaining the impossible, in dominating
experience, and in pursuing all vicious circles to
satisfactory conclusions.

> *I am the master of my fate;*
> *I am the captain of my soul!*

When the snake swallows his tail he has a swelled head. It is quite another thing to see that you are your "fate," and that there is no one either to master it or to be mastered, to rule or to surrender.

Must we also insist that this loss of "I" in God is not a mystic miasma in which the "values of personality" are obliterated? The "I" was not, is not, and never will be a part of human personality. There is nothing unique, or "different," or interesting about it. On the contrary, the more human beings pursue it, the more uniform, uninteresting, and impersonal they become. The faster things move in circles, the sooner they become indistinguishable blurs. It is obvious that the only interesting people are interested people, and to be completely interested is to have forgotten about "I."

We can see, then, that the basic principles of philosophy, religion, and metaphysics may be understood in two entirely different ways. They can be seen as symbols of the undivided mind, expressions of the truth that in each moment life and experience are a complete whole. "God" is not a definition of this state but an exclamation about it. Ordinarily, however, they are used as attempts to stand outside oneself and the universe to grasp them and to rule them. This process is circular, however complex and devious.

Because men have been circling for so many ages,

the powers of technology have availed for little save to speed the process to a point of unbearable tension. Civilization is ready to fly apart by sheer centrifugal force. In such a predicament the self-conscious type of religion to which we have so long been accustomed is no cure, but part of the disease. If scientific thought has weakened its power we need have no regrets, for the "God" to which it could have brought us was not the unknown Reality which the name signifies, but only a projection of ourselves—a cosmic, discarnate "I" lording it over the universe.

The true splendor of science is not so much that it names and classifies, records and predicts, but that it observes and desires to know the facts, whatever they may turn out to be. However much it may confuse facts with conventions, and reality with arbitrary divisions, in this openness and sincerity of mind it bears some resemblance to religion, understood in its other and deeper sense. The greater the scientist, the more he is impressed with his ignorance of reality, and the more he realizes that his laws and labels, descriptions and definitions, are the products of his own thought. They help him to use the world for purposes of his own devising rather than to understand and explain it.

The more he analyzes the universe into infinitesimals, the more things he finds to classify, and the more he perceives the relativity of all classification.

What he does not know seems to increase in geometric progression to what he knows. Steadily he approaches the point where what is unknown is not a mere blank space in a web of words but a window in the mind, a window whose name is not ignorance but wonder.

The timid mind shuts this window with a bang, and is silent and thoughtless about what it does not know in order to chatter the more about what it thinks it knows. It fills up the uncharted spaces with mere repetition of what has already been explored. But the open mind knows that the most minutely explored territories have not really been known at all, but only marked and measured a thousand times over. And the fascinating mystery of *what* it is that we mark and measure must in the end "tease us out of thought" until the mind forgets to circle and to pursue its own processes, and becomes aware that to *be* at this moment is pure miracle.

In ways that differ but little, this is the last word of Western and Eastern wisdom alike. The Hindu *Upanishads* say:

> He who thinks that God is not comprehended, by him God is comprehended; but he who thinks that God is comprehended knows him not. God is unknown to those who know him, and is known to those who do not know him at all.

Goethe says it in words which, to the modern mind, may be plainer:

The highest to which man can attain is wonder; and if the prime phenomenon makes him wonder, let him be content; nothing higher can it give him, and nothing further should he seek for behind it; here is the limit.

Or there are the words of St. John of the Cross, one of the greatest seers of the Christian tradition:

One of the greatest favors bestowed on the soul transiently in this life is to enable it to see so distinctly and to feel so profoundly that it cannot comprehend God at all. These souls are herein somewhat like the saints in heaven, where they who know him most perfectly perceive most clearly that he is infinitely incomprehensible; for those who have the less clear vision do not perceive so clearly as do these others how greatly he transcends their vision.

In such wonder there is not hunger but fulfillment. Almost everyone has known it, but only in rare instants when the startling beauty or strangeness of a scene drew the mind away from its self-pursuit, and for a moment made it unable to find words for the feeling. We are, then, most fortunate to be living in a time when human knowledge has gone so far that it begins to be at a loss for words, not at the strange and marvelous alone, but at the most ordinary things. The dust on the shelves has become as much of a mystery as the remotest stars; we know enough of both to know that we know nothing. Eddington, the physicist, is nearest to the mystics, not in his airier flights of fancy, but when he says quite simply, "Something unknown is doing we don't know what."

In such a confession thought has moved full circle, and we are again as children. To those still feverishly intent upon explaining all things, upon securing the water of life firmly in paper and string, this confession says nothing and means nothing but defeat. To others, the fact that thought has completed a circle is a revelation of what man has been doing, not only in philosophy, religion, and speculative science, but also in psychology and morals, in everyday feeling and living. His mind has been in a whirl to be away from itself and to catch itself.

> *Ye suffer from yourselves, none else compels,*
> *None other holds you that ye live and die*
> *And whir upon the wheel, and hug and kiss*
>   *its spokes of agony,*
> *Its tire of tears, its nave of nothingness.*

Discovering this the mind becomes whole: the split between I and me, man and the world, the ideal and the real, comes to an end. *Paranoia,* the mind beside itself, becomes *metanoia,* the mind with itself and so free from itself. Free from clutching at themselves the hands can handle; free from looking after themselves the eyes can see; free from trying to understand itself thought can think. In such feeling, seeing, and thinking life requires no future to complete itself nor explanation to justify itself. In this moment it is finished.

ALAN W. WATTS, who held both a master's degree in theology and a doctorate of divinity, is best known as an interpreter of Zen Buddhism in particular, and of Indian and Chinese philosophy in general. Standing apart, however, from sectarian membership, he has earned the reputation of being one of the most original and "unrutted" philosophers of the century. He was the author of some twenty books on the philosophy and psychology of religion, including (in Vintage Books) *The Way of Zen; The Joyous Cosmology; Nature, Man, and Woman; Behold the Spirit; The Book; Does It Matter?; This Is It; The Supreme Identity; Beyond Theology;* and *Cloud Hidden, Whereabouts Unknown.* He died in 1973.